QUILTING AMONG FRIENDS

by Jill Reber

Landauer Books

Quilting Among Friends

Copyright© 2005 by Landauer Corporation
Projects Copyright© 2005 by Jill Reber

This book was designed, produced, and published by Landauer Books
A division of Landauer Corporation
3100 NW 101st Street, Urbandale, IA 50322

President/Publisher: Jeramy Lanigan Landauer
Director of Operations: Kitty Jacobson
Editor in Chief: Becky Johnston
Project Coordinator: Eve Mahr
Contributing Writer: Linda Hungerford
Creative Directors: Laurel Albright, Linda Bender
Technical Editor: Connie McCall
Technical Illustrator: Linda Bender
Photographer: Craig Anderson Photography

We also wish to thank Terry Clothier Thompson for permission to use her Rose of Sharon pattern (©Peace Creek Patterns, 1982), as the center medallion of the Bordering on Lessons Learned quilt featured on page 20.

Library of Congress Cataloging-in-Publication Data
Reber, Jill.
  Quilting among friends : 15 friendship quilts and 48 bonus blocks for quilting among friends with dozens of bee-friendly tips and ideas for fun swaps, exchanges, and retreats / by Jill Reber.-- 1st ed.
     p. cm.
ISBN: 1-890621-86-2
  1. Patchwork--Patterns. 2. Quilting. 3. Friendship quilts. I. Title.
TT835.R385 2005
746.46'041--dc22

                                                      2005040805

This book printed on acid-free paper.
Printed in China

                                      ISBN 13: 978-1-890621-86-5
10-9-8-7-6-5-4-3-2   ISBN 10:   1-890621-86-2

Introduction

Quilting among friends has been an American tradition since Colonial days. Prompted by scarcity, quilters have shared cherished fabric scraps with one another or regularly devoted hours to participating in quilting bees to meticulously create a quilt by hand. Whether gathered around a quilting frame or attending a guild meeting, quilters enjoy camaraderie—particularly with other quilters—and have created ingenious ways to encourage it.

Trading pieces through fabric exchanges, block swaps and showers, shared row quilts, or round robin quilts encourages quilters to expand their quilting skills. Sometimes the lesson learned from an exchange is as valuable as, for example, learning how to select colors that complement and contrast with one another.

During piecing times spent together or by sharing blocks, quilters may discover talent for creatively resolving a sewing concern or an under-utilized ability to figure quilting math.

Most of all, in the process of trading, piecing, and sharing, new friendships and deeper relationships are forged among quilters. Because quilters are ever ready to help and encourage one another and celebrate accomplishments, each person comes away with something—a little more know-how, sometimes a new (and special) quilt, and quilting friendships built on a foundation of shared experiences. On the following pages, master quilter Jill Reber shares with you 55 blocks to mix and match and 15 quilts to make, with dozens of bee-friendly tips and ideas for fun exchanges, swaps, and retreats so that you can discover your own joys of friendship quilting.

Becky Johnston, Editor

Quilting friends (from L to R), Cindy Ohmart, Jill Reber, and Julie Armstrong have a built a close relationship upon a love for quilting.

Jill Reber (seated left) and her Twisted Sisters quilting friends (back, L to R) Cindy Ohmart, Lynn Johnson, Peggy Warner, and (seated, L to R), Jill, Deanne Main, Diane Crawford and Julie Armstrong.

Foreword

by Jill Reber

For a dedicated quilter like me, it's satisfying to see the work of my hands result in a beautiful quilt. But even more delightful are the friendships that I've had the privilege of growing within my quilting circle. Something very special occurs among us when we're speaking the same quilt-making language, trading ideas that can lead from one creative thought to another, and sharing our personal lives—the everyday and special occasions we all experience. Sharing these things together helps us grow as quilters, affirms our relationships, and continues to make our group special to each individual.

This book has been prepared with a sincere hope that you and your quilting friends will forge similar enduring relationships. Within these pages you'll find the information, ideas, and inspiration that will guide you and your quilting friends toward building lasting friendships. Enjoy the path of discovery as you look for greater joy and purpose in your quilting. Enjoy the experience when you quilt among friends.

Contents

I appreciate that my quilting friends will share their time and talents with me. I consider their friendship a gift—something special that I wouldn't have without quilting in my life.

—Marcia Jacobs

It's rewarding to quilt with my friends. We not only accomplish things to be proud of, but we laugh and have fun while we're doing it.

—Deanne Main

My quilting friends are creative and they help me stretch myself—get out-of-the-box. Then, year after year I get to enjoy a wonderful quilt with unique designs.

—Char Rathbone

When I think about the quilts I have made with and for my friends, I remember everything going on during that time. Sometimes the memories make me laugh and sometimes they bring tears.

—Diane Crawford

TRADING PIECES

On the following pages you'll find photos, explanations, suggestions, and tips about how to organize and implement exchanges with your quilting friends.

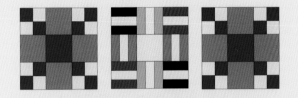

Fabric Exchanges
Projects: Swapping the Blues Quilt, Charmed Child Quilt, Bordering on Lessons Learned Quilt

Block Swap
Projects: Framed Setting, Attic Windows Setting

Block Shower
Projects: Strippy Setting, On-Point Setting

Row Quilts

Round Robin
Project: Summertime Quilt

Fabric Exchanges

In a fabric exchange, a group of quilting friends swap same-sized fabric yardages or pieces with one another. Fabric swapping can be based on favorite color and print preferences, and on what block designs and quilt patterns might be made with the traded fabrics.

How Fabric Exchanges Works

A group of quilting friends swap same-sized fabric yardages or pieces with one another. Fabric swapping can be based on favorite color and print preferences, and what block designs and quilt patterns might be made with the traded fabrics.

Getting Started

Toss around ideas and possibilities within your group. What size will the traded pieces be? What fabric color, type, or theme will we trade? Base your swap on one or more of the following considerations:

Size

The size of the fabric you swap may depend on the ultimate use of the fabric. Consider whether you're just collecting fabrics to build your inventory, or whether particular-sized pieces will be used to make a specific quilt pattern. Will you trade yardage amounts, or a particular-size cut piece? For a yardage trade, swap as little as 1/8 yard or as much as a yard. A fat quarter (18" x 22") is an easy size to trade because they can be readily purchased. Deciding whether to swap cut pieces, such as 6" squares or 2-1/2" strips, may depend upon the quilt pattern you've decided to make.

Consider trading pieces of fabric that have been cut from a manufactured acrylic template. Templates are available in a variety of shapes such as assorted sizes of triangles, Tumbler, Dresden Plate, and Grandmother's Flower Garden. They're easy to cut out and easy to swap. Just make sure each participant cuts fabric by using the same size and brand of template.

Color

Perhaps your quilting friends want to expand their collections of red, blue, green, or neutral colors.

Type

Choose from batiks, prairie prints, homespuns, and reproduction fabrics, including Civil War prints or 1930s prints.

Theme or Subject Matter

Swapping fabrics printed with chickens, or with sports equipment, flowers, leaves, fruit, or sewing notions, can lead to several fun quilts. How about a chocolate-themed trade?

Pattern

Stripes, plaids or solid colors are interesting swap options that can lead to spectacular quilts. A swap of solid colors is a good way to collect fabrics for that Amish style quilt you've always wanted to make.

Also decide whether the quilter will determine for herself how she's going to use her fabric, or whether everyone will make a quilt following the same pattern. Determine when the trade will occur.

Once decisions are agreed upon, make sure everyone knows the information. Clear communication about what fabrics are being exchanged and when the exchange will occur

---

Fabric Exchange Ideas

How About Trading...

1/4-yard pieces of yellow floral prints

•

5" squares of indigo prints

•

2-1/2" strips of dark, country prints

•

1930s reproduction fat quarters

•

9" x 22" rectangles of homespun fabrics

•

1/2 yard of a novelty print, cut into two fat quarters. Keep one; trade one.

Fabric Exchange Quilt
Swapping the Blues

"My quilting friends know that my favorite color is blue. On my 40th birthday, they gave me 40 different 1/4-yard pieces so I wouldn't forget what day it was. From the fabrics I made 'My 40th Birthday Blues' that reminds me of my best decade yet!"

Swapping the Blues

The clues are in the blues, in colors and values reflecting the sky and water. With fabrics collected in an exchange, you too can create movement-filled quilts like this one.

Materials

Finished size is 90" x 108"
Yardage is based on 100 percent cotton fabric that is at least 42" wide.

40 assorted 1/4-yard strips of blue prints for blocks and outer border

40 assorted 4" x 42" strips (or 4-1/2 yards) of mottled tan prints for blocks

1 yard of mottled tan for inner border

3/4 yard of navy blue for binding

Batting to fit the finished quilt top

5-3/4 yards of backing, seamed to fit

Cutting Instructions

A 1/4" seam allowance is included in these measurements.

From each of the 40 strips of blue prints , cut:
6 squares 3-7/8" x 3-7/8"; cut each square in half diagonally to make 12 half-square triangles (total of 480)

3 squares 3-1/2" x 3-1/2" (120 total)

Also from the blue prints, cut:
124 rectangles 3-1/2" x 6-1/2" for outer border

From each of the 40 mottled tan print strips, cut:
6 squares 3-7/8" x 3-7/8"; cut each square in half diagonally to make 12 half-square triangles (480 total)

3 squares 3-1/2" x 3-1/2" (120 total)

From the mottled tan for the inner border, cut:
9 strips 3-1/2" x 42"

From the navy blue for the binding, cut:
10 strips 2-1/2" x 42"

Assembling the Quilt

Quilt Center

1. Pair each set of 12 blue print half-square triangles and 3 blue print squares with a set of 12 mottled tan print half-square triangles and 3 mottled tan print squares.

2. Sew each of the 12 blue half-square triangles to a mottled tan half-square triangle, as shown. Make 12 triangle squares from each set, and set aside 6 of them.

3. Arrange 6 triangle squares and 3 blue squares as shown. Sew them into 3 rows, and then sew the rows together to make an A Block. Make 40.

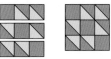

4. Arrange the other 6 triangle squares and 3 mottled tan print squares as shown. Sew them into 3 rows, and then sew the rows together to make a B Block. When all 40 blue/tan sets are sewn into blocks, you will have 40 A Blocks and 40 B Blocks.

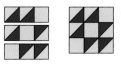

5. Alternating A Blocks and B Blocks, arrange the finished blocks in 10 rows of 8 blocks, as shown. Sew them into rows, and then sew the rows together.

Inner Border

For the inner border, use the 3-1/2" x 42" strips of mottled tan.

1. Sew 2 of the 3-1/2" x 42" mottled tan strips together. Trim to 72-1/2", and sew them to the top and bottom of the quilt center.

2. Cut a 3-1/2" x 42" rectangle in half, and sew each half to two full-length strips. Trim to 96-1/2", and sew them to the sides of the quilt center.

Outer Border

For the outer border, use the blue print 3-1/2" x 6-1/2" rectangles.

1. Select 26 blue print rectangles, and sew them together randomly in a strip, as shown. Make 2.

2. Sew the strips of 26 rectangles to the top and bottom of the quilt center. Press the seams toward the tan inner border.

3. Select 36 blue print rectangles, and sew them together randomly in a strip, as shown. Make 2.

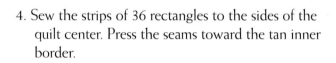

4. Sew the strips of 36 rectangles to the sides of the quilt center. Press the seams toward the tan inner border.

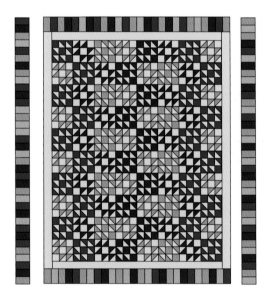

Finishing the Quilt

1. Layer the backing, the batting, and the quilt top.

2. Baste the layers together. Hand- or machine-quilt as desired.

3. Bind the quilt with the 2-1/2" x 42" navy blue strips (see General Instructions).

Swapping the Blues Finished Quilt Assembly

Fabric Exchange Quilt
Charmed Child

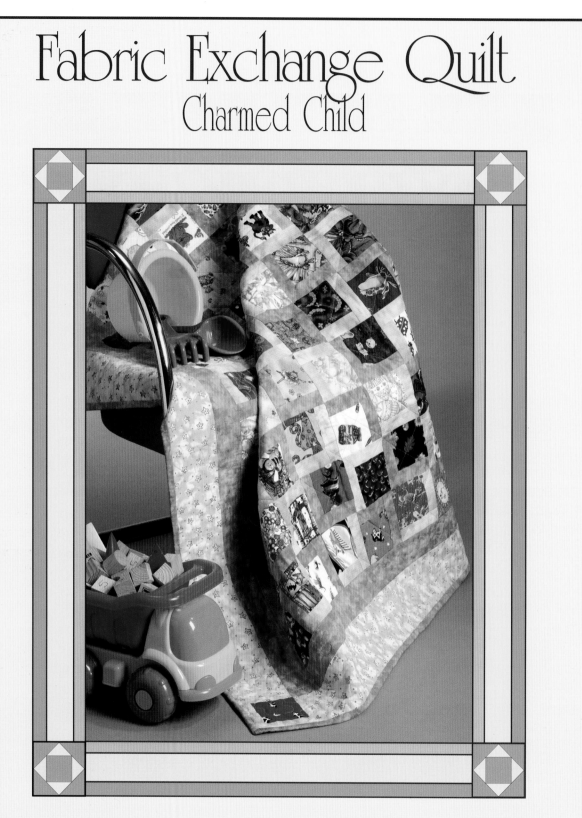

"When little ones visit the Reber household, they nap or build forts with this quilt. It's fun to play 'I Spy' too. We search for frogs, fish, cats, and other characters hidden in the assorted prints."

Charmed Child

Cheerful and charming small qu[...]
a child's eyes. Trading charm sq[...]
tradition that can be shared by[...]

4. Arrange [...] as [...]

Materials

Finished size is 44" x 60".
Yardage is based on 100 percent cotton fabric
that is at least 42" wide.

100 assorted 3-1/2" squares of bright pictorial prints

1-1/2 yards of mottled gold for frames,
inner border, and binding

5/8 yard of mottled blue for frames

3/4 yard of small print for outer border

Batting to fit finished quilt top

3 yards of backing, seamed to fit

Cutting Instructions

A 1/4" seam allowance is included in these measurements.

From the mottled gold, cut:
 2 strips 3-1/2" x 42" for frames; from
 these strips, cut
 50 rectangles 1-1/2" x 3-1/2"

 2 strips 4-1/2" x 42" for frames; from
 these strips, cut
 50 rectangles 1-1/2" x 4-1/2"

 5 strips 2-1/2" x 42" for inner border; from
 these strips, cut
 2 strips 2-1/2" x 32-1/2" for inner border
 top and bottom, and
 3 strips 2-1/2" x 42" for inner border sides

 6 strips 2-1/2" x 42" for binding

From the mottled blue, cut:
 2 strips 3-1/2" x 42" for frames; from
 these strips, cut
 50 rectangles 1-1/2" x 3-1/2"

 2 strips 4-1/2" x 42" for frames; from
 these strips, cut
 50 rectangles 1-1/2" x 4-1/2"

From the small print, cut:
 5 strips 4-1/2" x 42" for outer border; from these
 strips, cut
 2 strips 4-1/2" x 36-1/2" for outer border and
 3 strips 4-1/2" x 42" for outer border

Assembling the Quilt

Quilt Center

1. Sew a gold 1-1/2" x 3-1/2" rectangle to the bottom of a 3-1/2" pictorial print square. Press seam toward the square. Sew a gold 1-1/2" x 4-1/2" rectangle to the right edge. Make 50.

2. In the same manner, sew the blue rectangles to the remaining 3-1/2" pictorial print squares. Make 50.

3. Sew 2 gold framed blocks and 2 blue framed blocks together as shown. Make 24. (Save the 4 remaining framed blocks for the outer border.)

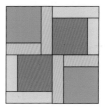

24 blocks into 6 rows of 4 blocks each shown. Sew them into rows. Sew the rows together.

Inner Border

1. Sew a gold 2-1/2" x 32-1/2" strip to the top and bottom of the quilt center. Press seams toward the border.

2. Cut a gold 2-1/2" x 42" strip in half, and sew each half to a full-length strip. Trim to 52-1/2", and sew to the sides of the quilt center. Press seams toward the border.

Outer Border

1. Sew a small-print 4-1/2" x 36-1/2" strip to the top and bottom of the quilt center. Press seams toward the outer border.

2. Cut a small-print 4-1/2" x 42" strip in half and sew each half to a full-length strip. Trim to 52-1/2". Sew one of the remaining framed blocks to each end of each strip. Press seams toward the outer borders.

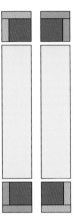

3. Sew the outer borders to the sides of the quilt center.

Finishing the Quilt

1. Layer the backing, the batting, and the quilt top.

2. Baste the layers together. Hand- or machine-quilt as desired.

3. Bind the quilt with the gold 2-1/2" x 42" strips (see General Instructions).

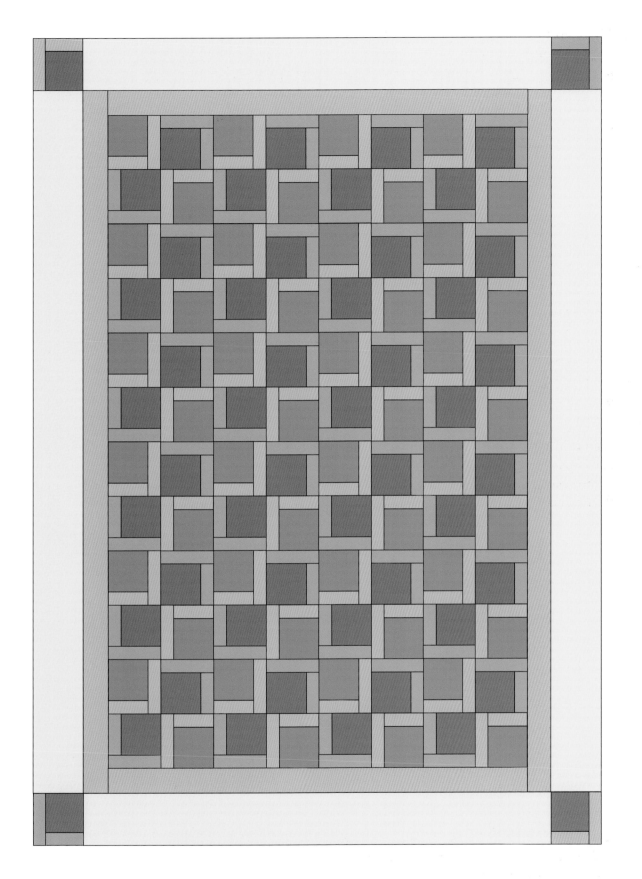

Charmed Child Finished Quilt Assembly

Fabric Exchange Quilt
Bordering on Lessons Learned

"After attending a Terry Thompson class about women and household fabrics they used during the Civil War era, two quilting friends joined me in making blocks for this fabric study using reproduction fabrics. It was a wonderful way to share a history lesson."

Bordering on Lessons Learned

Romantically reminiscent of times past, a simple design created in muted colors begins with a lovely piece of appliqué. Surround it with blocks made with fabric exchanged by quilting friends.

Materials

Finished size is 64" x 64"
Yardage is based on 100 percent cotton fabric that is at least 42" wide.

1 Whig Rose appliquéd square (see page 22) or another 36-1/2" square

64 rectangles 2-7/8" x 18" in 64 different dark prints for blocks

1-1/2 yards of cream print for blocks

1/2 yard of brown print for binding

Batting to fit the finished quilt top

4 yards of backing, seamed to fit

Cutting Instructions

A 1/4" seam allowance is included in these measurements.

From each of the 64 dark print rectangles, cut:
2 squares 2-7/8" x 2-7/8"; cut squares in half diagonally to make 4 half-square triangles, a total of 256

Trim the remainder of each dark print rectangle to 2-1/2" wide, and cut:
4 squares 2-1/2" x 2-1/2"

From the cream print, cut:
128 squares 2-7/8" x 2-7/8"; cut squares in half diagonally to make 256 half-square triangles

64 squares 2-1/2" x 2-1/2"

From the brown print, cut for binding:
7 strips 2-1/2" x 42"

Quilt Border

Making the Shoofly Blocks

1. Sew a dark half-square triangle to a cream half-square triangle to make a triangle square. Press the seams toward the dark fabric. Make 4 triangle squares of each dark print.

2. Arrange 4 matching triangle squares, 4 dark squares, and a cream square as shown. Sew together in rows, and sew the rows together to make a Shoofly Block. Make 64.

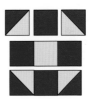

Assembling the Border

1. Randomly arrange the 64 blocks in groups of 4. Sew each group together as a unit.

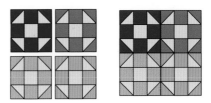

2. Sew 3 units together as shown. Make 2, and sew them to the top and bottom of the quilt center.

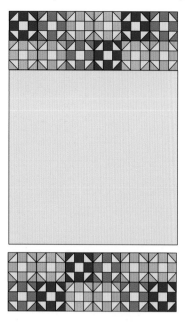

3. Sew 5 units together as shown. Make 2, and sew them to the sides of the quilt center.

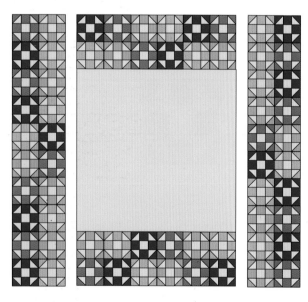

Finishing the Quilt

1. Layer the backing fabric, the batting, and the quilt top.

2. Baste the layers together. Hand- or machine-quilt as desired.

3. Bind the quilt with the 2-1/2" strips of brown print.

Whig Rose Appliqué

Materials

1-1/8 yards of tan print for background

1/2 yard of dark green solid for vine

1 fat quarter (18" x 22") of red print for blossoms

Scraps of gold, green, red, and blue prints

Note: The Whig Rose appliqué shown here is used with permission from Terry Thompson of Peace Creek Patterns.

Cutting Instructions

A 1/4" seam allowance is included in these measurements.

From the tan print, cut:
1 square 40" x 40"

From the dark green solid, cut:
2-1/2"-wide bias strips to equal 2-1/2 yards for vine

From the red print, cut:
4 of the Rose template

From scraps of two blue prints, cut:
1 of the Center template

1 of the Center Ring template

From the gold, green, and red, scraps, cut:
4 of each remaining template

Adding the Appliqués

1. Sew the bias strips together in one long strip for the vine. Fold the bias strip into thirds lengthwise.

2. Trace the appliqué templates from pages 24-25, and cut them out. Refer to General Instructions to prepare pieces for appliqué.

3. Using the picture as a guide, arrange the appliqué pieces and the sections of vine on the tan square.

4. Hand- or machine-appliqué.

5. Center the appliqués, and trim the square to 36-1/2".

Bordering on Lessons Learned Finished Quilt Assembly

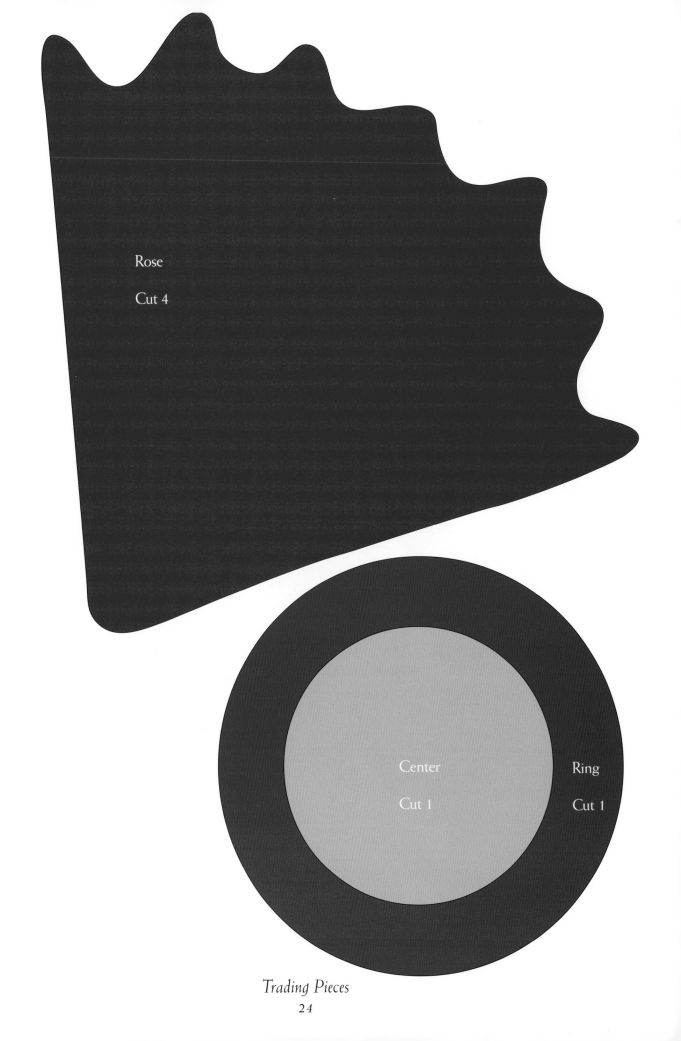

Rose

Cut 4

Center

Cut 1

Ring

Cut 1

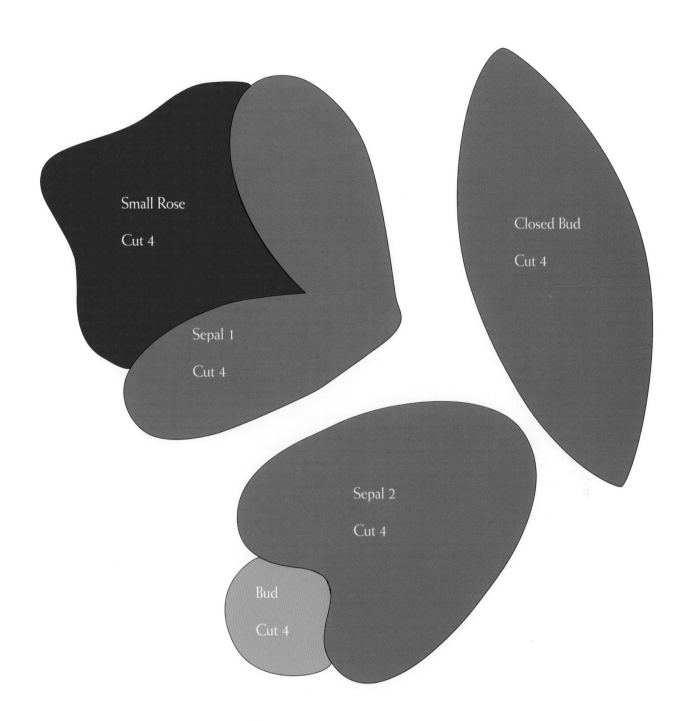

Small Rose

Cut 4

Sepal 1

Cut 4

Closed Bud

Cut 4

Sepal 2

Cut 4

Bud

Cut 4

Block Swap

Each quilter makes one block design, repeatedly, for every quilter within her group. It's often decided that at the conclusion of the block swap, each quilter may set her blocks according to the pattern of her choice.

Getting Started

Several key decisions must be made before you begin. Here are some questions to spark creative block swaps within your group:

How many quilters will participate?

Consider your group's size. Then, plan to make one block for yourself and one block for every quilter in your group. Having at least one block from each quilting friend is what makes block-swap quilts special. Agree on how many blocks everyone is willing to make.

What block design will we make?

Hundreds of block designs are available. Pieced blocks and appliquéd blocks work equally well. Refer to the Block Gallery and then try this:

Make two different blocks. Groups with quilters at different skill levels may decide to have half of the group make pieced blocks while the other half makes appliquéd blocks. Allow each quilter to make any block design she chooses as long as the design is the required size.

What size blocks should we make?

Whether you decide to make 4" blocks or 14" blocks, make sure everyone in your group knows both the unfinished dimension and the finished dimension of the block you agree to make. Try this:

Make blocks that finish at 12", 15" or 18" if your group has six or fewer participants.

Make 4" or 6" finished blocks in groups with 20 or more quilters.

Make your blocks in a specified size, but allow quilters to make their block design choices.

What fabric palette will we use?

As when trading fabrics, you'll need to decide whether your block swap will be based on a color scheme, a particular print, or a theme. For example, make blocks using only two prints, or sew blocks from a variety of country-colored prints with a variety of ivory background prints. Make blocks from leaf prints and cream-colored background prints. Choose a holiday and make blocks in appropriate colors or prints. This might be a good time to start a Christmas quilt or a Halloween wallhanging. Other block swap palette ideas include: Batiks, Brights, Pastels, Patriotic and Reproduction prints.

When will blocks be due?
When will our swap conclude?

As with all types of exchanges, be sure everyone knows how frequently your block swap will occur, the dates when blocks will be exchanged, and how the exchange will happen. While most block swaps occur face-to-face, some are by mail. Check the Internet for Web sites that coordinate block swaps by mail, or organize one among your long-distance friends. Remember to document whatever your quilting friends agree to and provide that information to everyone. Participants will more clearly understand what's expected, and will be able to meet due dates.

Block Swap Tips

Give swapped blocks a unified appearance by having each quilter use the same background fabric. Purchase 1-1/2 yards to 2 yards per person.

•

Decide whether or not block fabrics will be pre-washed. An agreement reached now may prevent heartache later.

•

Even though we all strive for the perfect quarter-inch seam allowance, the reality is that each of us sews a little differently. When setting your collected blocks into a quilt top, consider choosing a setting that "forgives" the variations in each person's unfinished block dimensions. For example, if you find yourself with unfinished blocks that measure from 12" to 12-1/2", make the 1/2" to 1" adjustment by adding sashing strips to all the blocks. After framing each block with sashing strips, trim blocks to a consistent size. Settings for 12" and 6" finished blocks are found on pages 29 and 33.

Block Swap Quilt
Framed Setting

"What fun we had making this quilt from the calendar month each of us drew from a hat. Now, every month, my 'Calendar Quilt' reminds me of another of my 11 very special friends."

Framed Setting

*Expressions of friendship may not be equal in size.
When swapped blocks don't quite match up,
cut the frame fabrics extra wide and trim to make
them all the same size.*

Materials

*Finished size is approximately 66" x 80"
Fabrics are based on 100% cotton fabric that
is at least 42" wide*

12 completed Cypress (see Blocks to Share) or other blocks,
12-1/2" square including seam allowance

12 sets of assorted dark prints for block frames
cut into 3" x 42" strips

Assorted scraps of dark prints for Four Patch border
and binding

Assorted scraps of light prints for Four Patch border

1 yard of mottled tan print for first and third borders

1-1/4 yards of golden brown print for outer border

Piece of batting to fit the finished top

6 yards of fabric for backing, seamed to fit

Cutting Instructions

A 1/4" seam allowance is included in these measurements.

From each of 12 sets of assorted dark prints, cut:
   2 rectangles 1-1/2" x 12-1/2" for block frames

   2 rectangles 1-1/2" x 14-1/2" for block frames

From the dark print scraps, cut:
   114 squares 2-1/2" x 2-1/2" for Four Patch border

   9 yards of 2-1/2" strips of random length
   for binding

From the assorted light print scraps, cut:
   114 squares 2-1/2" x 2-1/2" for Four Patch border

From the mottled tan print, cut:
   6 strips 2-1/2" x 42" for first border

   7 strips 2-1/2" x 42" for third border

From the golden brown print, cut:
   7 strips 4-1/2" x 42" for outer border

Framing the Blocks

1. Sew one pair of dark print 1-1/2" x 12-1/2" rectangles to the top and bottom of a completed block. Sew the matching 1-1/2" x 14-1/2" rectangles to the sides of the block. Press seams toward the rectangles. Repeat the process to make 12 framed blocks.

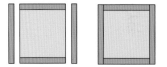

2. Arrange the blocks in rows of three, making four rows. Sew each of the four rows, and then sew the rows together to complete the quilt center. Press as directed in the General Instructions.

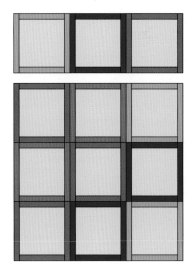

Adding the Borders

First Border

1. Cut one 2-1/2" x 42" mottled tan strip in half to make two strips 2-1/2" x 21". Sew each of these half-strips to a full-length strip, and trim the resulting rectangles to 42-1/2". Sew the rectangles to the top and the bottom of the quilt top. Press seams toward the border.

2. Cut another 2-1/2" x 42" mottled tan strip in half to make two strips 2-1/2" x 21". Sew each of these half-strips to a full-length strip. Trim the resulting rectangles to 60-1/2", and sew them to the sides of the quilt top. Press seams toward the border.

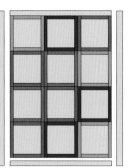

Second Border (Four Patch)

1. Sew the dark 2-1/2" squares and the light 2-1/2" squares together in random pairs, as shown. Make 114 pairs. Press seams toward the dark squares.

2. Set two of the pairs aside. Sew the remaining pairs together to make 56 Four Patch units. Press all of the seams in the same direction.

3. Sew 11 Four Patch units together in a row, and then sew one of the reserved pairs to one end of the row. Make 2 rows, and sew them to the top and bottom of the quilt center. Press the seams toward the quilt center.

4. Sew 17 Four Patch units together in a row. Make 2 rows, and sew them to the sides of the quilt center. Press the seams toward the center.

Third Border

1. Cut one 2-1/2" x 42" mottled tan strip in half to make two strips 2-1/2" x 21". Sew each of these half-strips to a full-length strip, and trim the resulting rectangles to 54-1/2". Sew the rectangles to the top and the bottom of the quilt top. Press seams toward the border.

2. Sew the remaining 2-1/2" x 42" mottled tan strips together in pairs, and trim the resulting rectangles to 76-1/2". Sew the rectangles to the sides of the quilt top. Press seams toward the border.

Outer Border

1. Cut one 4-1/2" x 42" golden brown strip in half to make two strips 4-1/2" x 21". Sew each of these half-strips to a full-length strip, and trim the resulting rectangles to 58-1/2". Sew the rectangles to the top and the bottom of the quilt top. Press seams toward the border.

2. Sew the remaining 4-1/2" x 42" golden brown strips together in pairs, and trim the resulting rectangles to 80-1/2". Sew the rectangles to the sides of the quilt top. Press seams toward the border.

Finishing the Quilt

1. Layer the backing fabric, the batting, and the quilt top.

2. Baste the layers together. Hand- or machine-quilt as desired.

3. Sew the random-length 2-1/2"-wide dark print strips together end to end, and use them to bind the edges of the quilt (see General Instructions).

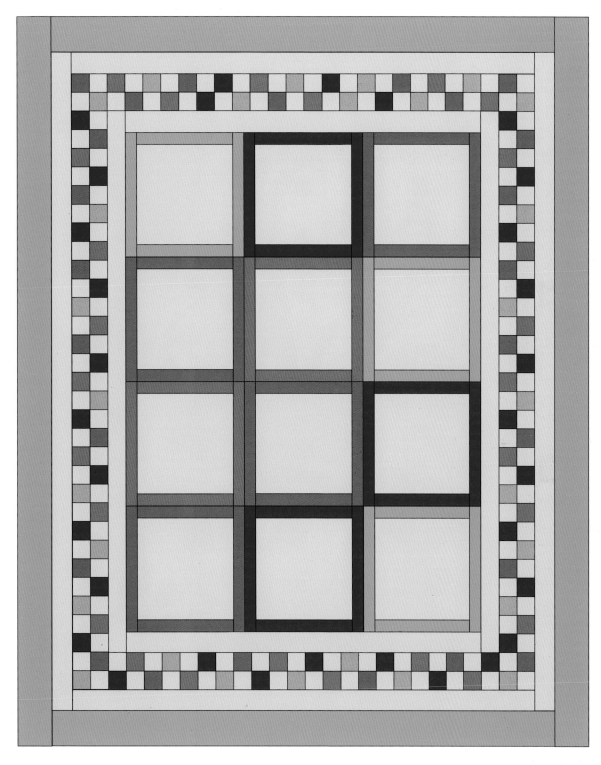

Framed Setting Finished Quilt Assembly

Block Swap Quilt
Attic Windows Setting

"The 48 blocks in this quilt mark an entire year of quilting creativity. 'The Four Seasons of Friendship' reminds me of the four friends whose personalities are reflected in all of the blocks."

Attic Windows Setting

Gaze upon an assortment of blocks through the windows of an old-fashioned block setting accented by a wide border that accommodates your favorite appliqué.

Materials

Finished size is approximately 76" x 92"
Yardage is based on 100 percent cotton fabric that is at least 42" wide.

48 completed blocks 6-1/2" square including seam allowance

1-1/2 yards of tan check for sashing and border

2 yards of navy for sashing, border, and binding

1-1/4 yards of mottled tan for appliquéd border

Scraps of assorted dark and tan prints for Four Patch border and outer border

Batting to fit the finished quilt top

6 yards of backing, seamed to fit

Note: For the appliquéd border, choose a design that coordinates with the friendship blocks.

Cutting Instructions

A 1/4" seam allowance is included in these measurements.

From the tan check, cut:

48 rectangles 2-1/2" x 9" for Attic Windows sashing

4 strips 2-1/2" x 42" for Attic Windows border

From the navy, cut:

48 rectangles 2-1/2" x 9" for Attic Windows sashing

4 strips 2-1/2" x 42" for Attic Windows border

9 strips 2-1/2" x 42" for binding

From the mottled tan, cut:

7 strips 6-1/2" x 42" for appliquéd border

From assorted scraps of dark prints, cut:

128 squares 2-1/2" x 2-1/2" for Four Patch border

Enough 2-1/2"-wide strips of random lengths to equal 350" (almost 10 yards)

From assorted scraps of tan prints, cut:

128 squares 2-1/2" x 2-1/2" for Four Patch border

Quilt Assembly

Adding the Attic Windows Sashing

1. Mark the 1/4" seam allowance at the lower left-hand corner of one of the completed blocks. Aligning the top edges, sew a navy 2-1/2" x 9" rectangle to the left side of the block, starting and stopping with backstitches at the 1/4" mark. Press seam toward the block.

2. Aligning the right-hand edges, sew a tan check 2-1/2" x 9" rectangle to the bottom edge of the block, starting and stopping with backstitches at the 1/4" mark. Press the seam toward the block.

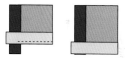

3. Fold the block diagonally, wrong side out, aligning the outer edges and seams of the navy and tan check rectangles. Draw a diagonal line from the 1/4" mark to the outer edge of the rectangles. Sew on the marked line, starting and stopping with backstitches at the mark. Trim the diagonal seam to 1/4". Press the diagonal seam open. Press the remaining seams toward the rectangles. Repeat Steps 1 to 3 for each of the 48 blocks.

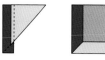

4. Arrange the blocks in 8 rows of 6 blocks each. Sew them into rows, and then sew the rows together.

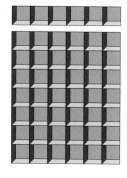

Adding the Attic Windows Border

1. Mark the 1/4" seam allowance at each corner. Sew 2 tan check 2-1/2" x 42" strips together. Repeat to make a second long strip. Sew one strip to the left-hand edge of the quilt center, starting and stopping with backstitches and allowing at least 3" to extend beyond the 1/4" mark. In the same manner, sew the second long tan check strip to the top edge.

2. Sew 2 navy 2-1/2" x 42" together. Repeat to make a second long strip. In the same manner as with the tan check strips, sew one navy strip to the right-hand edge and the other to the bottom edge.

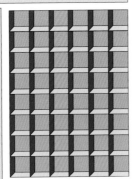

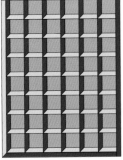

3. In the same manner as with the Attic Windows tan check and navy sashing, miter the upper right-hand and lower left-hand corners.

Adding the Four Patch Border

1. Select 2 dark 2-1/2" squares and 2 light 2-1/2" squares, and sew them together as shown. Make 64 Four Patch units.

2. Sew 13 Four Patch units into a row. Repeat to make a second row of 13. Sew these rows to the top and bottom edges of the quilt center.

3. Sew 19 Four Patch units into a row, and repeat to make a second row of 19. Sew these rows to the side edges of the quilt center.

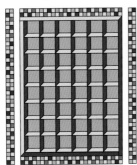

Adding the Tan Border

1. Cut one mottled tan 6-1/2" x 42" strip in half, and sew each half to a full-length strip. Trim these strips to 60-1/2", and sew them to the top and bottom of the quilt center. Press seams toward the border.

2. Sew the remaining mottled tan strips together in pairs. Trim them to 76-1/2" and sew them to the sides of the quilt center. Press seams toward the border.

Adding the Outer Border

1. Sew dark print 2-1/2"-wide strips together end to end to make 2 strips 72-1/2" in length. Sew them to the top and bottom of the quilt center. Press seams toward the quilt center.

2. Sew the remaining strips together end to end to make 2 strips 92-1/2" in length. Sew them to the sides of the quilt center. Press seams toward the quilt center.

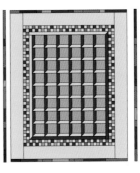

Finishing the Quilt

1. Add appliqués to the tan border, as desired.

2. Layer the backing fabric, the batting, and the quilt top.

3. Baste the layers together. Hand- or machine-quilt as desired.

4. Bind the quilt with the 2-1/2" x 42" navy strips (see General Instructions).

Trading Pieces

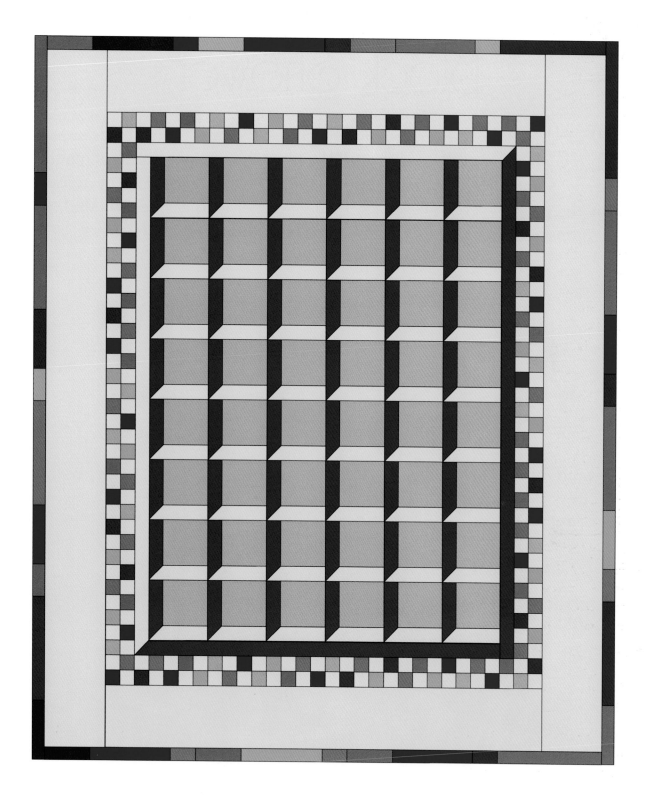

Attic Windows Finished Quilt Assembly

Block Shower

A block shower, also referred to as a block party, differs from a block swap in that one quilter is the recipient of all the blocks made by a group of quilting friends. Sometimes, none of the blocks in the finished quilt have been made by the quilt owner; however, it's the quilt owner who decides whether to make additional blocks, how the blocks should be put together, and what setting, sashings, and borders she prefers.

Getting Started

A group of quilters may decide to organize a block shower for a number of reasons:

Birthdays

•

Anniversaries

•

Congratulations on a new home or a new job

•

Birth of a child or grandchild

•

Retirement

•

A move or going-away

•

A thank-you for a job well done

Quilting friends may also decide to have a block shower lottery. This activity is simply for the fun of taking a chance to win many blocks. For a lottery, your group should select a block, determining the design, size, and color to make. Then, for every block a quilter makes and places into a "pool," she'll receive the same number of chances to have her name picked to win all the blocks.

A Surprise Shower

A block shower requires as much planning as a block swap, particularly if you want the recipient to be surprised. Determine how many quilters will make blocks and how many blocks you want to shower. Then, make decisions about block design, block size, color and/or theme palette and when blocks are due.

When you've reached agreement, be sure to document and share with everyone what you've decided. Communicating these decisions will help every participant enjoy the experience.

Planned Showers for Each Quilter

Over the course of a year, rotate until each quilter receives a block shower. In turn, allow each quilter in your group to decide for herself what block design, block size and fabric or theme she wants to receive from every other quilter within her group. The block shower recipient may also provide the pattern, and some or all of the fabric from which blocks should be made.

Block Shower Tips

To avoid misunderstandings, discuss these potential questions before they arise:

•

Should fabrics be pre-washed before being sewn into blocks?

•

Should blocks be signed or initialed?

Also, strive to sew your blocks into the agreed-upon unfinished size. Because each quilter sews a little differently, variances in quarter-inch seams may result in blocks that do not meet the required dimensions.

Block Shower Quilt
Strippy Setting

"Members of the Des Moines Area Quilters Guild showered me with 'dark country colors' of Friendship Star blocks after my first term as the guild's quilt show chair. Some blocks are signed and include sentiments. I was lucky to receive enough blocks to make an entire quilt!"

Strippy Setting

A stunningly simple yet striking star design attracts your eyes to the strips in this vertically-pieced quilt—a perfect setting for many blocks.

Materials

Finished size is 72" x 96"
Yardage is based on 100 percent cotton fabric that is at least 42" wide.

95 Friendship Star blocks (for instructions see page 40) or other blocks, 6-1/2" square including seam allowance

2-1/4 yards of mottled blue print for sashing and binding

1/2 yard of mottled gold print for inner border

1-1/2 yards of blue floral print for outer border

Batting to fit the finished quilt top

6 yards of backing, seamed to fit

Cutting Instructions

A 1/4" seam allowance is included in these measurements.

From the mottled blue print, cut:

19 strips 2-1/2" x 42" for sashing

9 strips 2-1/2" x 42" for binding

From the mottled gold print, cut:

7 strips 1-1/2" x 42" for inner border

From the blue floral print, cut:

7 strips 6-1/2" x 42" for outer border

4 rectangles 1-1/2" x 6-1/2" for edging corner blocks

4 rectangles 1-1/2" x 7-1/2" for edging corner blocks

Assembling the Quilt

Quilt Center

1. Sew 13 blocks into a row. Make 7 rows. (Save the 4 remaining blocks for the border.)

2. Sew 2 mottled blue 2-1/2" x 42" strips together and trim to 78-1/2". Make 8. Sew between the block rows and along the sides as shown. Press seams toward sashing.

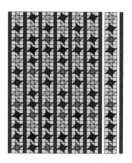

3. Cut a mottled blue 2-1/2" x 42" strip in half, and sew each half to a full-length strip. Trim to 58-1/2", and sew to the top and bottom of the quilt center. Press seams toward the sashing.

Borders

1. Cut a mottled gold 1-1/2" x 42" border strip in half, and sew each half to a full-length strip. Trim to 58-1/2", and set them aside.

2. Cut a blue floral print 6-1/2" x 42" border strip in half, and sew each half to a full-length strip. Trim them to 58-1/2".

3. Sew the long edges of the gold and blue border strips together, and sew them to the top and bottom of the quilt top.

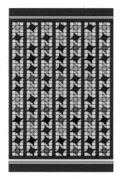

4. Sew 2 gold 1-1/2" x 42" strips together, and trim to 80-1/2". Make 2, and set them aside.

5. Sew 2 blue floral 6-1/2" x 42" strips together, and trim them to 80-1/2". Make 2, and set them aside.

6. Sew a blue floral print 1-1/2" x 6-1/2" rectangle to the top edge of each of the 4 remaining blocks as shown. Sew a blue floral print 1-1/2" x 7-1/2" rectangle to an adjoining side of each block—on the right-hand side of 2 of the blocks and on the left-hand side of the other 2 blocks.

7. Sew the gold and the blue border strips together. Sew one of the 4 blocks to each end of each border, as shown, and sew the borders to the sides of the quilt top.

Finishing the Quilt

1. Layer the backing, the batting, and the quilt top.

2. Baste the layers together. Hand- or machine-quilt as desired.

3. Bind the quilt with the remaining 2-1/2" strips of mottled blue fabric (see General Instructions).

Friendship Star Block

Materials

3" x 16" strip of tan for background

3" x 9" strip of dark print

Cutting Instructions

A 1/4" seam allowance is included in these measurements.

From the tan background strip, cut:
2 squares 2-7/8" x 2-7/8"; cut the squares in half diagonally to make 4 half-square triangles

4 squares 2-1/2" x 2-1/2"

From the dark print, cut:
2 squares 2-7/8" x 2-7/8", and then cut the squares in half diagonally to make 4 half-square triangles

1 square 2-1/2" x 2-1/2"

Piecing the Block

1. Sew a tan triangle to a dark print triangle to make a triangle square. Make 4.

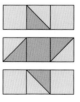

2. Arrange the triangle squares, the tan squares, and the dark print square as shown, and sew them together into 3 rows. Sew the 3 rows together to complete the Friendship Star block.

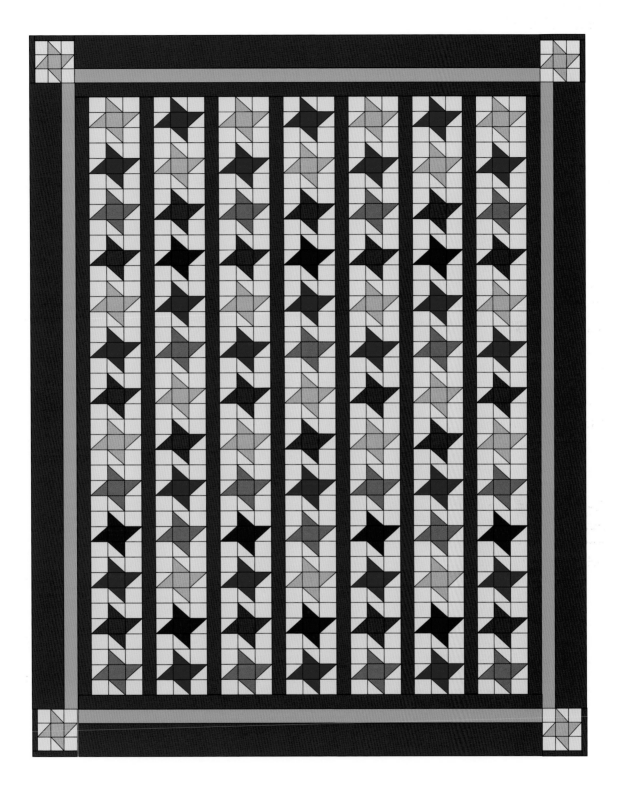

Strippy Setting Finished Quilt Assembly

Trading Pieces

Block Shower Quilt
On-Point Setting

"These sweet quilts were put together with blocks traded with my friend Cindy. We each collected an assortment of 1930s reproduction fabrics and made identical blocks to trade with one another. My quilt is set in yellow and blue colors while Cindy chose pink and purple."

On-Point Setting

Baskets show to perfection when placed on point. Use this setting when you've collected a limited number of blocks, but you want to make a larger quilt.

Materials

Finished size is approximately 55" x 46"
Yardage is based on 100 percent cotton fabric that is at least 42" wide.

20 completed Basket blocks, or others, 6-1/2" square including seam allowance

1 yard of yellow solid for setting blocks

1 yard of light blue solid for inner border and binding

1 yard of blue print for outer border

Batting to fit finished quilt top

3 yards of backing, seamed to fit

Cutting Instructions

A 1/4" seam allowance is included in these measurements.

From the yellow solid, cut:

12 squares 6-1/2" x 6-1/2"

4 squares 7-1/4" x 7-1/4"; cut these squares in half diagonally twice to make 16 quarter-square triangles (you will use only 14)

2 squares 5-1/2" x 5-1/2"; cut these squares in half diagonally once to make 4 half-square triangles

From the light blue solid, cut:

5 strips 2" x 42" for inner border

3 strips 2-1/2" x 42" for binding

From the blue print, cut:

5 strips 6" x 42" for outer border

Assembling the Quilt Top

Quilt Center

1. Arrange the basket blocks, solid yellow squares, and solid yellow triangles as shown.

2. Sew together in diagonal rows. Sew the rows together.

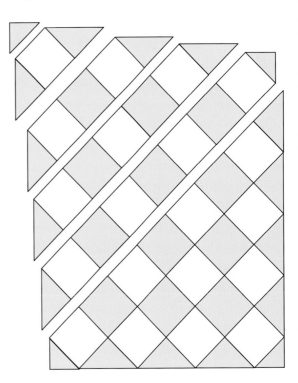

Inner Border

1. Measure the width of the quilt center at the top and bottom. (If necessary, average the two widths.) Trim 2 light blue 2" x 42" strips to this width, and sew them to the top and bottom of the quilt center. Press seams toward the border.

2. Cut one 2" x 42" strip in half, and sew each half to a full-length strip. Measure the length of the quilt center at each side. (If necessary, average the two lengths.) Trim each strip to this length, and sew them to the sides of the quilt center. Press seams toward the border.

Outer Border

1. Measure the new width of the quilt at the top and bottom. (If necessary, average the two widths.) Trim 2 floral print 6" x 42" strips to this width, and sew them to the top and bottom of the quilt center. Press seams toward the outer border.

2. Cut one 6" x 42" floral print strip in half, and sew each half to a full-length strip. Measure the new length of the quilt center at each side. (If necessary, average the two lengths.) Trim each strip to this length, and sew them to the sides of the quilt center. Press seams toward the outer border.

Finishing the Quilt

1. Layer the backing fabric, the batting, and the quilt top.

2. Baste the layers together. Hand- or machine-quilt as desired.

3. Bind the quilt with the light blue 2-1/2" x 42" strips (see General Instructions).

Basket Block

Materials

(for one block)

6" x 12" scrap of small print A for basket handle, interior, and base, or 4" x 7" scrap for basket interior and base

2" x 12" or 4" x 6" scrap of small print B for basket exterior, or 9" x 6" scrap for basket handle and exterior

6" x 12" scrap of solid white for background

Heat-resistant template plastic or cardboard

Cutting Instructions

A 1/4" seam allowance is included in these measurements.

From small print A, cut:

1 square 3-7/8" x 3-7/8"; cut in half diagonally to make 2 half-square triangles (you will use only 1)

1 square 2-7/8" x 2-7/8"; cut in half diagonally to make 2 half-square triangles (you will use only 1)

From small print B, cut:

1 of Template B

1 of Template B reversed

From small print A or B, cut:

1 bias strip 1-1/2" x 7" for handle

From the solid white, cut:

1 square 5-7/8" x 5-7/8"; cut in half diagonally to make 2 half-square triangles (you will use only 1)

1 square 2-7/8" x 2-7/8"; cut in half diagonally to make 2 half-square triangles (you will use only 1)

2 rectangles 1-1/2" x 4-1/2"

Piecing the Basket Block

Making the Handle

1. Trace Template A on template plastic and cut it out.

2. Wrong sides together and using a 1/8" seam allowance, sew the long edges of the 1-1/2" x 7" bias strip together to form a tube.

3. Slide the tube onto the template, center the seam allowance on the back, and press with steam.

4. Slide the tube off the template, and center it on the white half-square triangle as shown. Hand- or machine-appliqué it into place to form the handle.

Making the Basket

1. Sew the small print A half-square triangles and the white 2-7/8" half-square triangles together to make a triangle square.

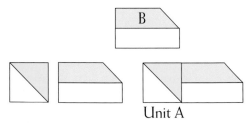

2. Sew the Template B piece to a white rectangle as shown. Sew the unit to the triangle square to make an A unit.

B

Unit A

3. Sew the Template B reversed piece to a white rectangle. Sew the unit to the small print A 3-7/8" half-square triangle to make a B unit.

Unit B

4. Sew the A unit to the B unit, as shown, to complete the basket unit. Sew the basket unit to the handle unit.

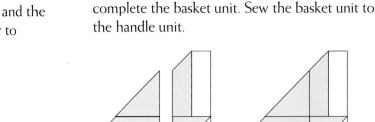

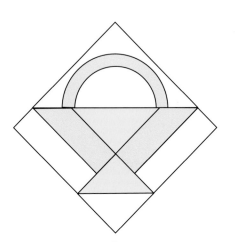

Template B
Cut 1
Cut 1 reversed

Template A
Handle

Trading Pieces

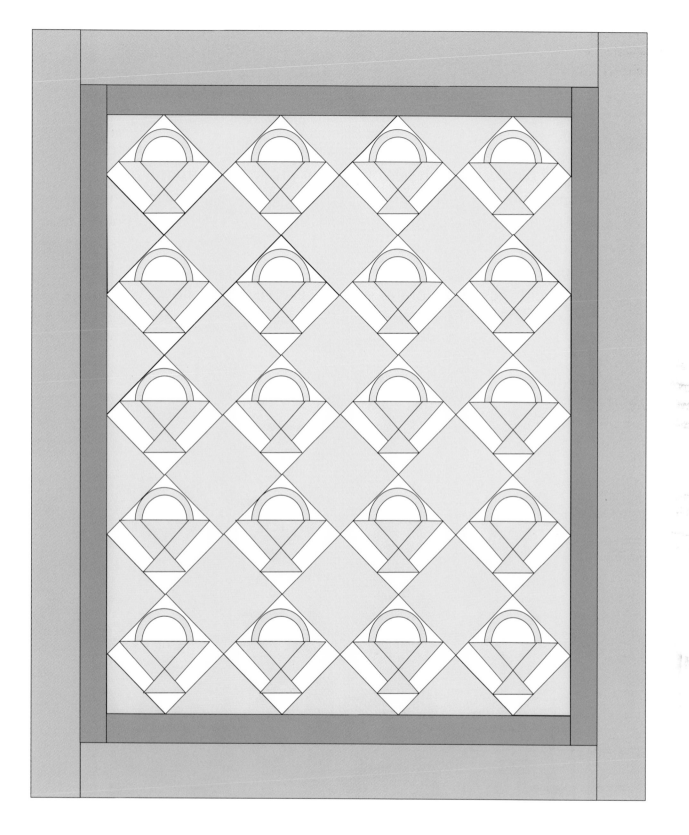

On-Point Setting Finished Quilt Assembly

Row Quilts

A row quilt exchange consists of sewing together a row of pieced or appliquéd blocks for each person in your group. As a group you'll make decisions about the row width, and perhaps the row height. Individually, each row quilt owner determines her own theme and colors. The owner may choose to include one or more fabrics in her "pass box" that rotates through participants. Many decisions need to be made, and it's decidedly helpful to document these decisions as rules for everyone to follow. As a group, quilters should agree upon the row size, how often you'll meet, and dates when rows must be completed.

Getting Started

Begin by brainstorming among your quilting friends. Toss around ideas, even if they sound outrageous. The fun develops when friends play off one another's great ideas, so let your imagination soar. Once you've considered every idea, make your decisions as a group, based on the elements listed below.

Size

Agree upon the width of each row; and make this your first group rule. A common row width is 60"; however, you may choose to make rows the same width as a fabric is sold—42" to 45"—and later add borders. Just keep in mind that the width you choose to make your finished quilt may necessitate making particular sized blocks or inserting fabric spacers (for example, sashing) to make the row the required width.

Also decide whether each row needs to be a specific height. While allowing row-makers to sew rows in whatever height they choose allows more freedom, an unspecified row height may result in a quilt that has grown out-of-hand. Consider this: If six quilters participate in the row exchange, and each row is made of five 12" blocks, you'll end up with a 60" x 72" quilt, not including borders.

Individually, each quilter should select a theme and colors, and should decide whether to include some specified fabric for each row.

Color

Once your theme has been chosen, it may dictate a particular color palette. For example, spring garden rows are pastels or jewel tones; Northwoods cabin rows are country colors; fall or harvest-time rows are browns, oranges and golds; and patriotic rows will be made from red, white, and blue fabrics. Clarify as much as possible. Should a spring garden include 1930s reproduction fabrics? Should houses be sewn from batiks?

Theme

Choosing the theme for your row quilt is where your creativity should soar. You need not make identical quilts! In fact, it's more fun for the row-maker to sew, and the quilt owner to receive, rows for a quilt with a particular theme. Here are some suggestions:

My garden

My farmyard

My Northwoods cabin

Fall or harvest time

My neighborhood, houses or other buildings

Amish life

Stars

Patriotic

Holiday – Halloween, Christmas, Easter

All About Me

For All About Me, base your theme on all or part of your first name or last name. Or, choose a physical characteristic or aspect of your personality that can be turned into a quilt that's a reflection of who you are.

Fabric

Create uniformity in the finished quilt by including in a pass box one or more fabrics to be used in each row. For example, a multi-colored focus fabric is helpful to include because it provides continuity and gives each quilter several options for accent colors. Each quilt owner may provide some fabric for her own row quilt, though it's generally agreed that the row-maker will also purchase fabrics or use her own fabrics.

Row Quilt Rules

When all decisions have been agreed upon, write rules that apply to the entire group, including whether to pre-wash fabrics. Discuss the importance of accurate 1/4" seams. Keeping everyone apprised of what's expected will ensure that each quilter has a positive experience.

•

Determine the pass box sequence. For example, pass alphabetically, by first or last name, or pass according to geographic location. It's helpful to create a chart that's a visual reminder of the passing sequence.

Row Quilt

Here's an example of a 60" star-studded row quilt made from blocks found on pages 115-132 and set together with 2" finished strips.

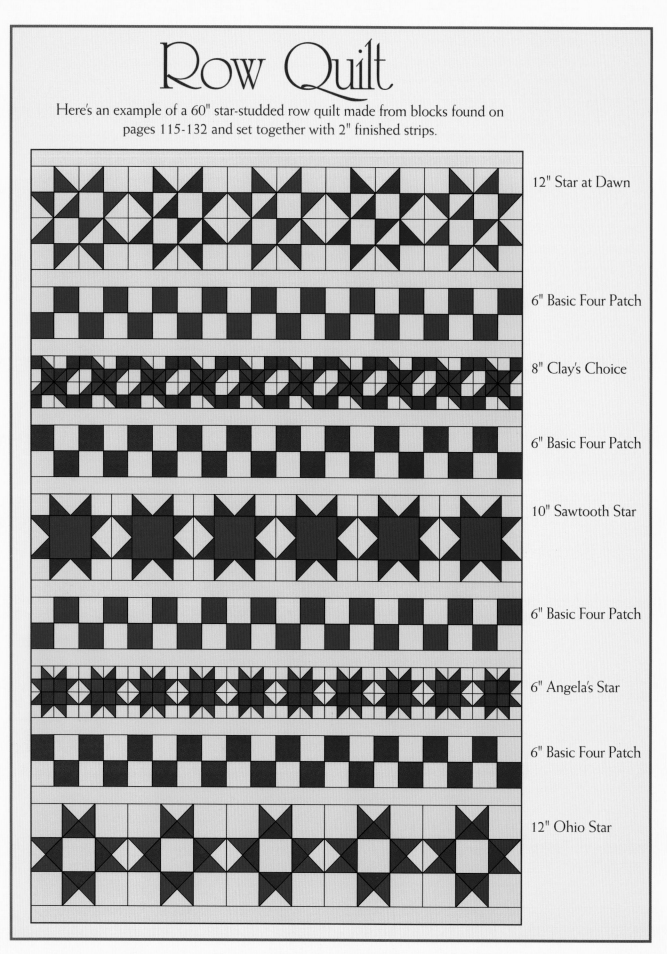

12" Star at Dawn

6" Basic Four Patch

8" Clay's Choice

6" Basic Four Patch

10" Sawtooth Star

6" Basic Four Patch

6" Angela's Star

6" Basic Four Patch

12" Ohio Star

Both Row quilts and Round Robin quilts (see page 56) require a little more planning and rule-making to ensure a successful outcome. While quilters at most skill levels will enjoy making these types of quilts, everyone should begin such an activity with an "I'm willing to learn" attitude.

Rules about sizes and sewing accuracy can make row quilts somewhat more challenging than simply sewing together a block; however, if you and your quilting friends are ready to branch out, coordinate a little extra planning, and meet a few more requirements, be assured that you'll learn, have fun, and experience the satisfaction of meeting a challenge.

Consider This:

Will the owner's rows be returned to her so she can decide the order in which they will be sewn together? Or, will each row be sewn to the next one, as the rows are passed along?

•

Is it acceptable to simply cut one piece of fabric the dimension of one row and apply appliqués?

•

Will completed rows be kept secret from the owner? Or, will rows be revealed as they are finished?

•

How often will we meet? When will each row be due?

•

Will we conclude our row exchange with a celebration such as a potluck or dessert party?

•

Will we display our finished quilts together at a special event?

Row Quilt Tips

Allow each quilt owner to write one or more rules about her rows—for example, "No hearts" or "No purple fabrics." Then abide by those preferences.

•

Quilt owners should provide a container or "pass box" in which individual rules, fabrics, completed rows, and a journal can be stored and transported.

•

Put a journal in your pass box so comments can be written about each row-maker's experience. For example, add your insights: "While making this I learned . . ." or "This row was inspired by . . ." Be sure to sign and date your comments. It's definitely a plus if quilters add photos of themselves and/or the rows they create.

•

Determine the pass box sequence. For example, pass alphabetically or by first or last name, or based on geographic location. It's helpful to create a chart that's a visual reminder of the passing sequence.

Round Robin

If you're comfortable making blocks and you've already participated in a row quilt project, you're probably ready for a new challenge. A round robin quilt can be the next progressive step, and it is usually recommended for experienced quilters. However, a less experienced quilter who has a positive attitude and a sincere desire to learn-as-you-go can also be successful. Each quilter should consider her own skill level, and plan to contribute good ideas and her best workmanship to a round robin exchange. Openness and interaction will help everyone learn through the experience. It's also very rewarding. In fact, you may learn that you liked it so much you'll want to try it again!

How a Round Robin Works

In turn, quilting friends add borders to a center block that has been made by the round robin quilt owner. Most commonly, in groups of eight or fewer quilters, borders are added to all four sides of a center block according to rules established before the sewing begins. Because the size of each round added to a round robin quilt is determined by the round made by the previous quilter, quilters who participate should:

1. Be familiar with how to select and make blocks or creative designs that complement previous rounds.
2. Expect to use some math, following basic principles about sizing blocks and patterns, to meet the particular dimensions of each round.

Getting Started

Key decisions need to be made both as a group and individually. Make group decisions about size, techniques for each round, and due dates. Make individual decisions about color and whether the round robin quilt should follow a theme. When all decisions are agreed upon, document them. Not only will this information remind everyone of what's expected, but when you're working on someone else's quilt, you'll know her preferences.

Group Decisions

Begin by making group decisions about:

Size

How small or large do you want finished round robin quilts to be? Discuss possible sizes for the block design that will be the quilt center. Block designs from 10" to 14" work well because they are large enough to be the focal point of the finished quilt. Added rounds should not overwhelm the center square. Plan to make rounds in a width that can be divided into the size of the center square. For example, add a 3"-, 4"-, or 6"-wide round to a block center that's 12" square. Groups with eight or more participants may find that adding four sides on each pass results in a quilt that's too large. Such large groups may decide that it is enough to add only two sides on a round.

Techniques

When choosing techniques to apply to each round, consider creating contrast. For example, if the center block is pieced, contrast that angularity with a first round of curves. Or, contrast a triangle round with appliqué. Options for rounds include rectangles, squares, curved piecing, foundation paper piecing, appliquéd blocks, whole border appliqué, or a combination of piecing and appliqué. Also be sure to choose shapes and techniques that challenge quilters to attempt techniques new to them and provide opportunities for particular quilting skills to shine.

As a group, review your preferences about whether to use pre-washed or unwashed fabrics in your quilts. When you reach consensus, write the rule and then abide by it. Also discuss the importance of accurate seam allowances, good workmanship, and each quilter's responsibility to put her best efforts into each round. The appearance of the round you add depends on the workmanship of the quilter who added a round before you.

Consider these questions and write group rules based on the answers:

Approximately how large will the finished quilt be?

•

Will every round robin owner make the same size center square? Should the square be a pieced block? Is an appliquéd center square acceptable?

•

Will rounds be added to all four sides of the center square? Or will a round consist of adding fabric to two adjoining sides? Which two?

•

Will each quilt owner provide fabric? How many fabrics and how much of each?

•

Will there be rules for every round?

•

Will the quilt be kept a secret from the round robin quilt owner?

•

How will we celebrate at the conclusion? Will we have a "revealing" party?

•

At what event can we display together our finished quilts?

Consider This

Here is an example of technique rules for a six-person round robin:

•

ROUND ONE
Round robin owner's choice

•

ROUND TWO
pieced squares

•

ROUND THREE
set the entire piece on point

ROUND FOUR
appliqué

•

ROUND FIVE
pieced triangles

•

ROUND SIX
"anything goes"

•

ROUND SEVEN
Round robin owner's choice

Individual Decisions

Individually, the owners of round robin quilts should make decisions about:

Color

Color choices in a round robin exchange are most important to the visual success of a round robin quilt. Because each round takes its design and color cues from the center block be sure to make a block that will stand strongly as the focal point of your quilt. The block should include several colors that other quilters can repeat throughout your quilt's multiple rounds. It's helpful if you include several pieces of fabric with your center block, as it makes its rounds. Each quilter should also expect to purchase additional fabric or use fabrics from her inventory for one another's rounds.

Theme

Because the center design dictates the style of each consecutive round, you may decide to choose a theme block. Your options are as broad as your creativity. Consider one of these:

Flowers

Seasons

Amish

Holiday – Halloween, Christmas

All About Me

For All About Me, base your theme on all or part of your first name or last name. Or, choose a physical characteristic or aspect of your personality that can be turned into a quilt that's a reflection of who you are.

A Pass Box

Select a plastic or cardboard container into which you put:

Your center square

•

Rules including group rules, due dates, and personal preferences

•

Extra fabric(s)

•

A journal

Round Robin Quilt
Summertime

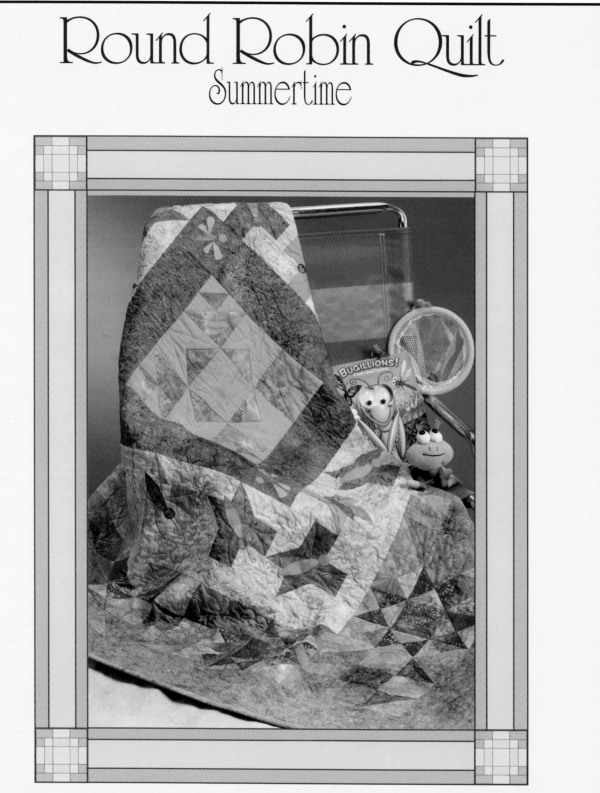

"This fun round robin exchange quilt represents everything that's special to me during the summer—I love to watch the dragonflies hover over the lake and to see the butterflies in my flower gardens. The batik fabrics are a perfect reflection of summer's clear colors."

Summertime

Breeze past the math often associated with round-by-round quilts. Share this 64" quilt as pictured, in your own fabric choices, or substitute equal-size blocks from Blocks to Share.

Round 1: Summer Winds Center Block

Materials

Finished size of block is 12" x 12"
Yardage is based on 100 percent cotton fabric that is at least 42" wide.

5/8 yard of bright yellow mottled batik

1 yard of blue-green mottled batik

Cutting Instructions

A 1/4" seam allowance is included in these measurements.

From the bright yellow batik, cut:

1 square 4-1/2" x 4-1/2"

4 rectangles 2-1/2" x 4-1/2"

10 squares 2-7/8" x 2-7/8"; cut these squares in half diagonally for 20 half-square triangles

From the blue-green batik, cut:

4 squares 2-1/2" x 2-1/2"

6 squares 2-7/8" x 2-7/8"; cut these squares in half diagonally for 12 half-square triangles

1 square 5-1/4" x 5-1/4"; cut this square in half diagonally twice for 4 quarter-square triangles

Piecing the Block

1. Sew 2 bright yellow half-square triangles to each blue-green quarter-square triangle as shown, to make 4 Flying Geese units. Press seams toward small triangles. Sew a bright yellow rectangle to each Flying Geese unit to make 4 A units.

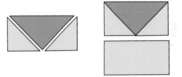

2. Sew each remaining bright yellow half-square triangle to a blue-green half-square triangle to make 12 triangle-squares.

3. Sew 3 triangle-squares and a blue-green square together as shown to make a B unit. Make 4.

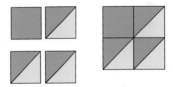

4. Arrange the bright yellow 4-1/2" square, the A units, and the B units as shown. Sew together in rows, and then sew the rows together.

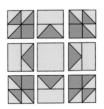

Round 2: Dragonfly Cornerstones and Sashing

Materials
Finished size of block is 4" x 4"

Batiks sent along from Round 1

1-1/2 yards of orange mottled batik

1/2 yard of medium green patterned batik

1 yard of medium blue patterned batik

Scraps of yellow and orange mottled batik

Cutting Instructions
A 1/4" seam allowance is included in these measurements.

From the orange batik, cut:
    4 of dragonfly body template

From the yellow batik, cut:
    4 of dragonfly head template

    8 each of dragonfly large wing template

    8 each of dragonfly small wing template

From the medium green batik, cut:
    4 squares 4-1/2" x 4-1/2"

From the medium blue batik, cut:

    4 rectangles 4-1/2" x 12-1/2"

Adding the Dragonfly Cornerstones and Sashing

1. Arrange the dragonfly body, head, 2 large wings and 2 small wings on each medium green square. Hand- or machine-appliqué (see General Instructions).

2. Sew a medium blue rectangle to the top and bottom of the center block. Press seams toward the rectangles.

3. Sew an appliquéd square to each end of the other 2 medium blue rectangles, and then sew one of the rectangles to each side of the center block. Press seams toward the rectangles.

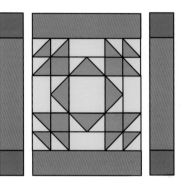

Round 2

Dragonfly template and assembly diagram

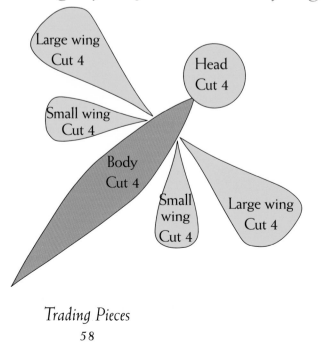

Round 3: Butterfly Blocks and Sashing

Materials

Finished size of block is 6" x 6"

Orange mottled batik, medium green patterned batik, medium blue patterned batiks from Rounds 1 and 2

1 yard of light blue mottled batik for background

Cutting Instructions

A 1/4" seam allowance is included in these measurements.

From each of the orange, medium blue, and medium green batiks, cut:

12 squares 2-1/2" x 2-1/2"

4 squares 2-7/8" x 2-7/8"; cut these squares in half diagonally for 8 half-square triangles.

4 of butterfly body template

4 of butterfly head template

From the light blue batik, cut:

60 squares 2-1/2" x 2-1/2"

16 squares 2-7/8" x 2-7/8" squares; cut in half diagonally for 32 half-square triangles

8 rectangles 1-1/2" x 6-1/2"

2 rectangles 2-1/2" x 32-1/2"

2 rectangles 22-1/2" x 36-1/2"

Adding the Butterfly Blocks

1. Sew an orange half-square triangle to a light blue half-square triangle to make a triangle square.

2. Arrange 3 bright yellow squares, 4 light blue squares, and 2 triangle squares as shown. Sew together in rows, and then sew the rows together. Make 4.

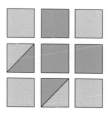

3. In the same manner, make 4 medium blue blocks, and 8 medium green blocks..

4. Arrange a butterfly head and body of contrasting color on each of the 16 blocks. Hand- or machine-appliqué (see General Instructions).

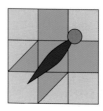

Round 3

Butterfly template and assembly diagram

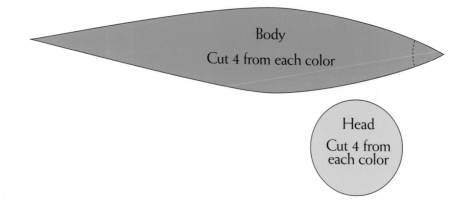

Body
Cut 4 from each color

Head
Cut 4 from each color

5. Place the 16 Butterfly blocks in rows, making 2 rows of 3 blocks and 2 rows of 5 blocks. In each row, insert a light blue 1-1/2" x 6-1/2" rectangle on each side of the middle Butterfly block, as shown. Sew each row together.

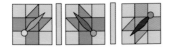

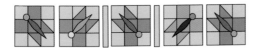

6. Sew a 3-block row to the top and bottom of the bordered center block, and sew a 5-block row to each side. Press seams toward the quilt center.

Adding the Sashing

1. Sew a light blue 1-1/2" x 32-1/2" rectangle to the top and bottom of the quilt center, and sew a light blue 1-1/2" x 36-1//2" rectangle to each side.

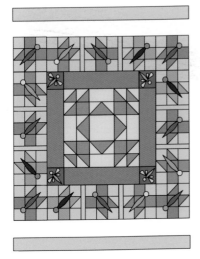

Round 4: Mystery Garden and Shoofly Blocks

Materials
Finished size of block is 9" x 9"

Batiks sent along from Rounds 1, 2, and 3

1/3 yard of light blue-and-rose mottled batik

5/8 yard of red-and-orange mottled batik

Cutting Instructions
A 1/4" seam allowance is included in these measurements.

From the medium blue batik, cut:
40 squares 3-1/2" x 3-1/2"

20 squares 3-7/8" x 3-7/8"; cut these squares in half diagonally for 40 half-square triangles

From the blue-and-rose batik, cut:
10 squares 4-1/4" x 4-1/4"; cut these squares in half diagonally twice for 40 quarter-square triangles

From the blue-green batik, cut:
10 squares 3-1/2" x 3-1/2"

20 squares 3-7/8" x 3-7/8"; cut these squares in half diagonally for 40 half-square triangles

From the orange batik, cut:
20 squares 4-1/4" x 4-1/4"; cut these squares in half twice for 80 quarter-square triangles

From the red-and-orange batik, cut:
10 squares 3-1/2" x 3-1/2"

20 squares 4-1/4" x 4-1/4"; cut these squares in half twice for 80 quarter-square triangles

Piecing the Blocks

Mystery Garden Block

1. Sew a medium blue quarter-square triangle and a blue-and-rose quarter-square triangle together as shown, to make a pieced half-square triangle. Press seams toward the medium blue. Make 40. Sew a pieced half-square triangle to a blue-green half-square triangle to make a triangle square. Press seams toward the blue-green.

2. Sew an orange quarter-square triangle to a red-and-orange quarter-square triangle as shown to make a half-square triangle. Press seams toward the red-and-orange. Make 80. Sew 2 half-square triangles together to make an hourglass unit. Make 40.

3. Arrange a red-and-orange square, 4 hourglass units, and 4 triangle squares as shown. Sew them into rows, and then sew the rows together. Make 10.

Shoofly Block

1. Sew a medium blue half-square triangle to a blue-green half-square triangle to make a triangle square. Press seams toward the medium blue. Make 40.

2. Arrange a medium blue square, 4 blue-green squares, and 4 triangle squares as shown. Sew them into rows, and then sew the rows together. Make 10.

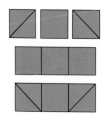

Adding the Blocks

1. Sew 2 Mystery Garden and 2 Shoofly blocks together, as shown. Make 2. Sew these units to the top and bottom of the quilt center.

2. Sew 3 Shoofly and 3 Mystery Garden blocks together, as shown. Make 2. Sew these units to the sides of the quilt center.

Round 5: Outer Border and Finishing

Materials

Orange mottled batik sent along from Round 2

1-1/4 yard of turquoise dragonfly patterned batik for borders

Batting to fit finished top

4 yards of backing, seamed to fit

Cutting Instructions

A 1/4" seam allowance is included in these measurements.

From the turquoise dragonfly patterned batik, cut:
   7 strips 5-1/2" x 42"

From the orange mottled batik, cut:
   7 strips 2-1/2" x 42"

Adding the Outer Border

1. Cut one 5-1/2" x 42" turquoise dragonfly border strip in half, and sew each half to a full-length strip. Trim borders to 54-1/2", and sew them to the top and bottom of the quilt center. Press seams toward the border.

2. Sew two 5-1/2" x 42" turquoise dragonfly border strips together, and trim border to 64-1/2". Make 2, and sew them to the sides of the quilt center. Press the seams toward the border.

Finishing the Quilt

1. Layer the backing, the batting, and the quilt top.

2. Baste the layers together. Hand- or machine-quilt as desired.

3. Bind the quilt with the orange 2-1/2"-wide strips (see General Instructions).

Summertime Finished Quilt Assembly

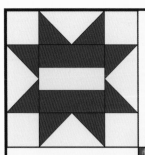

Quilting with friends makes me feel connected, like I'm a small part of a big sisterhood. My friends encourage me to try things I've never done before, and to be productive. I always have a happy anticipation about getting together with them.

—Cindy Ohmart

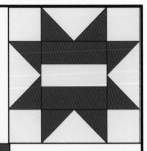

Looking back on the time I've spent with quilting friends, I recognize how I have grown as a quilt maker. And, my quilting relationships have brought us closer together. Each person is a meaningful part of my life.

—Jody Hamlin

When I think about the quilts I have made with and for my friends, I remember everything that was going on during that time. Sometimes the memories make me laugh and sometimes they bring tears.

—Diane Crawford

It means a lot to know how much thought quilting friends put into the quilts they make for me. They observe what I like and incorporate those details into a quilt, making it a mirror of my life.

—Peggy Warner

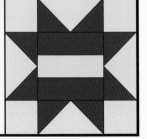

Piecing Times

PIECING TIMES

Numerous occasions call for the gift of a quilt. And a quilt is especially meaningful when it's created among friends. When quilters generously share their time and skills toward one effort, favorite people know they're remembered in a special way.

Charity and Children
Projects: Baby Coins Quilt, Fast & Fun Child's Quilt,
Four Patch Express Quilt

Retreats
Projects: Hen Party Quilt, Spool Spree Quilt

Milestone Quilts
Projects: Rings of Love Quilt, Birthday Bouquet Quilt

Charity & Children

In the spirit of giving, quilters often look for ways to share their time, talents, and creativity. One avenue is to organize quilting friends to make quilts for charitable organizations. Non-profit groups that provide services to infants, children, teens, or adults welcome quilts not only for their warmth, but for the homey, comfortable feeling they add to otherwise bare or sterile environments.

Quilt Patterns

Joining together to make quilts for others is one way that quilters share themselves. It happens time and again—when there's a special need, a crisis, or special children to be recognized, quilters are some of the first people to step forward, offering to contribute a quilt.

Getting Started

Begin by choosing a block design that's not only easy to sew, but that will allow quilters the freedom to interpret blocks differently by their color selections. Select more than one block design, if you'd like, but keep them simple for easier and faster construction.

Plan a Charity Quilt Project

Identify at least one other person to assist you in planning and carrying out the charity quilts project.

•

Identify an organization to receive your quilts. If it is appropriate, invite someone from that organization to speak to your group about why there's a need for quilts.

•

Determine whether quilts should be a particular size, or specifically for males or females.

•

Ask for donations. Invite quilters and non-quilters to donate 100 percent cotton fabrics, or money toward the purchase of materials. If asked, some quilting-related businesses will provide supplies or quilting services.

•

Plan one or more sewing days. Quilting friends will enjoy the chance to spend productive sewing time together.

•

Set a deadline for completing quilts and delivering them to the designated charity.

•

Take photos of completed quilts, and collect the names of the quilt-makers. Recognize quilters for their contributions in an appropriate manner.

Quilt Colors

When you are making quilts for adults, your pattern and color options may be dictated by gender. If it's possible, determine whether the intended quilt recipients are males or females. Baby quilts are most often made with fabrics that are pastel colors, bright novelty prints, or jewel tones.

Quilt Sizes

A baby quilt is an ideal project for a beginning quilter. The smaller size takes less time, and there's less investment in fabric. Baby quilts are appropriate for many places, including children's hospitals and church mission efforts. A lap quilt made in grown-up fabrics can be made for people confined to wheelchairs and for other adults who might appreciate a little extra warmth. A single bed-sized quilt is appreciated by youth centers, hospitals, and nursing homes.

Places Quilts Can Go

If you and your group of quilting friends decide you'd like to make quilts for a charitable organization, look for recipients within your own community. While it's wonderful to send quilts to other places, unless you can arrange free transportation, charges for freight or shipping can make it more costly to get your quilts into the recipients' hands. Local organizations that may welcome your quilt contributions include:

Cancer groups
•
Children's hospitals, neo-natal units
•
Group homes for adults with/without disabilities
•
Homeless centers
•
Homes for terminally ill children
•
Teen centers

Piecing Times

Charity Baby Quilt
Baby Coins

"Making a baby quilt is always a joy. They're simple and fast to sew, and they make a very special gift for a new little one. It was delightful to sew this quilt from the fabrics I collected in a fabric swap of 1930s reproduction prints."

Baby Coins

Stack 'em high! Show off a collection of your favorite fabric prints and colors to make this simple vertically-designed quilt with endless color possibilities.

Materials

Finished size is approximately 42" x 52"
Yardage is based on 100 percent cotton fabric that is at least 42" wide.

14 strips 2-1/2" x 42" of assorted small prints

5/8 yard of white solid for sashing

3/4 yard of pink small print for border

1/2 yard of blue solid for binding

Batting to fit the finished quilt top

2-1/2 yards of backing, seamed to fit

Cutting Instructions

A 1/4" seam allowance is included in these measurements.

From the assorted small prints, cut:
80 rectangles 2-1/2" x 6-1/2"

From the white solid, cut:
7 strips 2-1/2" x 42"

From the pink print, cut:
5 strips 4-1/2" x 42"

From the blue solid, cut:
5 strips 2-1/2" x 42"

Assembling the Quilt

Quilt Center

1. Randomly sew the small-print rectangles into rows of 20. Make 4.

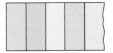

2. Trim 5 of the solid white sashing strips to 40-1/2". Sew 3 of them between the rows of small prints to join them. Sew the remaining 2 along the sides.

3. Trim the remaining solid white sashing strips to 34-1/2", and sew them to the top and bottom of the quilt center.

Border

1. Cut one of the pink print border strips in half, and sew each half to a full-length strip. Trim them to 44-1/2", and sew them to the sides of the quilt center.

2. Trim the remaining border pieces to 42-1/2", and sew them to the top and bottom of the quilt center.

Finishing the Quilt

1. Layer the backing fabric, the batting, and the quilt top.

2. Baste the layers together. Hand- or machine-quilt as desired.

3. Bind the quilt with the blue solid 2-1/2"-wide strips (see General Instructions).

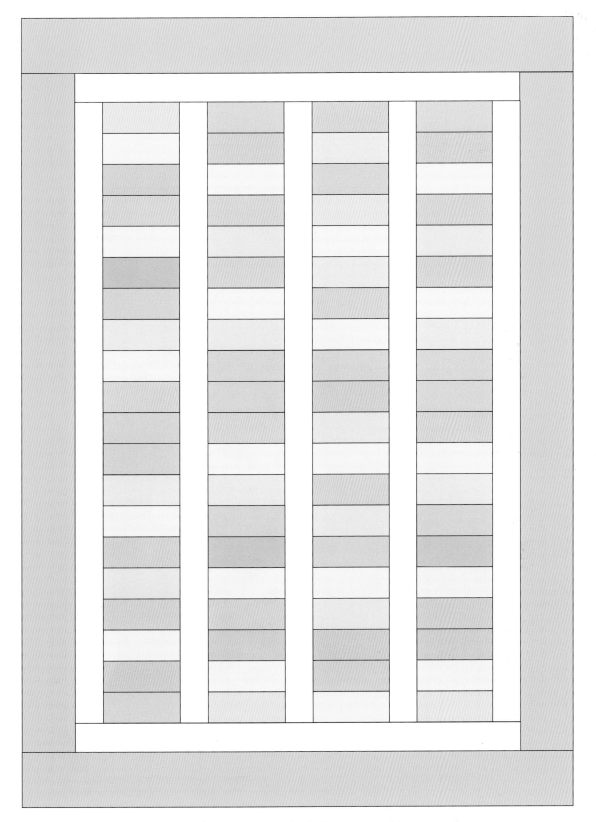

Baby Coins Finished Quilt Assembly

Charity Baby Quilt
Fast & Fun Child's Quilt

"By choosing a fun novelty fabric for the large center of this child-sized quilt you can put it together in an afternoon. Use a nice complementary fabric for the border, quilt it with sturdy machine-quilting, and you've got a great, go-anywhere quilt."

Fast & Fun Child's Quilt

It's a wagon full of fun! Let the child in you romp through the bright array of novelty print fabrics and choose something cheery to make a small quilt—fast!

Materials

Finished size is approximately 40" x 48"
Yardage is based on 100 per-cent cotton fabric that is at least 42" wide.

1 yard of large print for the quilt center

5/8 yard of coordinating print for the border

1/2 yard of fabric for binding (optional)

Batting to fit the finished quilt top

1-1/2 yards of backing

Cutting Instructions

A 1/4" seam allowance is included in these measurements.

From the large print, cut:
   1 rectangle 32-1/2" x 40-1/2"

From the coordinating border print, cut:
   2 rectangles 4-1/2" x 40-1/2"

   2 rectangles 4-1/2" x 42-1/2"

From the (optional) binding fabric, cut:
   2-1/2" strips to equal 4-1/4 yards total

Assembling the Quilt

1. Sew a 4-1/2" x 40-1/2" rectangle of the border print to each side of the center. Press seams toward the quilt center.

2. Sew a 4-1/2" x 42-1/2" rectangle of the border print to the top and bottom of the quilt center. Press seams toward the center.

Finishing the Quilt

1. Layer the backing fabric, the batting, and the quilt top.

2. Baste the layers together. Hand- or machine-quilt as desired.

3. Bind the quilt with the 2-1/2"-wide strips of binding fabric (see General Instructions).

Charity Baby Quilt
Four Patch Express

"'I think I can, I think I can' is all the encouragement you'll need to make this easy, pint-sized quilt. It's warm and cozy for snuggle-time story reading before a nap or bedtime."

Four Patch Express

Tootle through your fabrics and sew easy Four Patch blocks. Add some plain blocks to make this small quilt in infinite color and print combinations.

Materials

Finished size is approximately 40" x 56"
Yardage is based on 100 per-cent cotton fabric that is at least 42" wide.

1/2 yard of light print for small squares

1 yard of dark print for small squares and binding

7/8 yard medium print for large squares

3/4 yard of large print for border

Batting to fit the finished quilt top

1-3/4 yards of backing, seamed to fit

Cutting Instructions

A 1/4" seam allowance is included in these measurements.

From the light print, cut:
6 strips 2-1/2 x 42" for Four Patch blocks

From the dark print, cut:
6 strips 2-1/2" x 42" for Four Patch blocks

5 strips 2-1/2" x 42" for binding

From the medium print, cut:
6 strips 4-1/2" x 42"; from these strips, cut 48 squares 4-1/2" x 4-1/2"

From the large print, cut:
5 strips 4-1/2" x 42" for border

Assembling the Quilt

Quilt Center

1. Sew a light print strip to a dark one. Press seam toward the dark fabric. Make 6.

2. Cut the strips into 2-1/2" sections. Make 96.

3. Sew the sections together in pairs to make Four Patch units. Make 48 pairs.

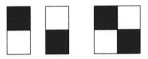

4. Sew 2 medium print 4-1/2" squares and 2 Four Patch units together to make a block. Make 24 blocks.

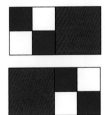

5. Arrange the blocks in 6 rows of 4 blocks each.

6. Sew the blocks into rows, and then sew the rows together.

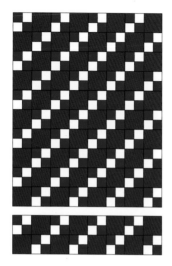

Border

1. Trim 2 large print 4-1/2" x 42" strips to 32-1/2". Sew them to the top and bottom of the quilt center. Press seams toward the quilt border.

2. Cut one of the large print 4-1/2" x 42" strips in half, and sew each half to a full-length strip. Trim them to 56-1/2", and sew them to the sides of the quilt center.

Finishing the Quilt

1. Layer the backing fabric, the batting and the quilt top.

2. Baste the layers together. Hand- or machine-quilt as desired.

3. Bind the quilt with the remaining 2-1/2"-wide dark print strips (see General Instructions).

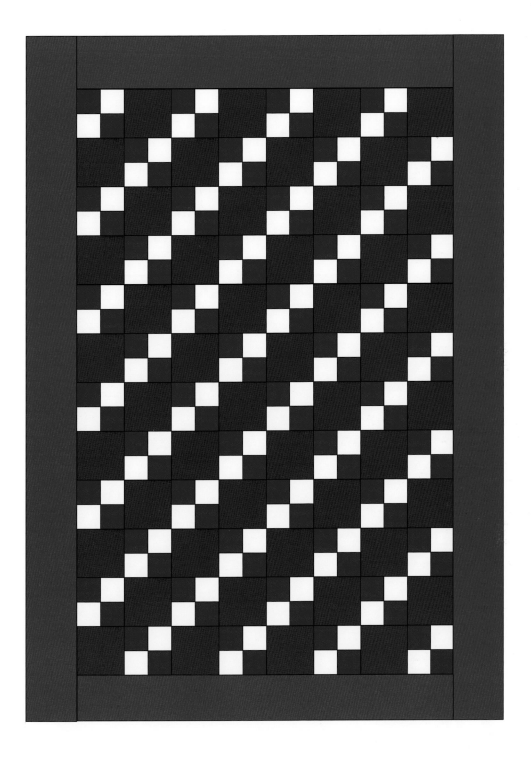

Four Patch Express Finished Quilt Assembly

Quilting Retreats

Whether your quilting friends want to plan a get-away to sew charity quilts together or to work on projects of their own, a retreat is an opportunity to leave your responsibilities behind and enjoy some quality sewing and friendship time. Ideally you should plan an overnight (or two!), but even a day retreat can give you the respite and sewing time you may find difficult to arrange at home.

Where

For a low-cost day retreat, arrange to gather at a quilting friend's home. Handy access to a kitchen and to forgotten sewing room supplies is a plus. However, if it's not possible to meet in a home, share the cost and reserve a room at a community center meeting room, a church, or a church camp.

Some quilt shops are now offering day retreat and overnight retreat facilities as part of their business. Because these retreat centers cater to quilters—sometimes providing sewing machines, access to fabric, catered food, or special classes—they can be more expensive, but they are no less enjoyable.

Overnight Retreats

If you'd prefer to stay overnight, or even two or three nights, you'll need a facility with beds, showers, and a kitchen. If you're willing to sleep in a sleeping bag instead of a bed, you may find more low-cost options available.

Theme

In addition to arranging the location, dates, times, and other details for your retreat, consider choosing a theme to make the event memorable. Though a theme isn't necessary, it can make the time you spend among quilting friends more entertaining and can help create special memories. The theme can even be carried through to a quilt pattern you decide to make while you're on retreat. Consider the many ways you can express your theme—in invitations, nametags, decorations, foods served, door prizes, and a quilt project.

Plan your retreat around one of these themes: Birthday, special era (Victorian, 1950s Retro, 1980s Disco), patriotic, season or holiday, a favorite book, a celebrity, baskets, a special place (city, lake, mountain), a sport, a collectors' item (Santas, snowmen, bird houses, teddy bears, antique dishes, cake stands, marbles, Barbie dolls).

Tips for a Successful Quilt Retreat

Enlist several quilters to help plan and implement the retreat.

•

Select a facility where people are willing to work with you.

•

Make sure the facility is wired for heavier-than-normal electrical demands. Irons and sewing machines use the most current.

•

Choose a theme and use it in all aspects of your retreat.

•

Plan easy-to-fix meals, or have meals prepared by people other than retreat-goers.

•

Provide an agenda so that retreat-goers know when it's time to sew, eat, and sleep.

•

Choose a retreat location that's near a quilt shop.

•

Have a retreat "show-and-tell" so everyone can see what others have worked on.

•

Keep a record of your plans and activities, in case you want to have a retreat again.

Retreat Quilt
Hen Party

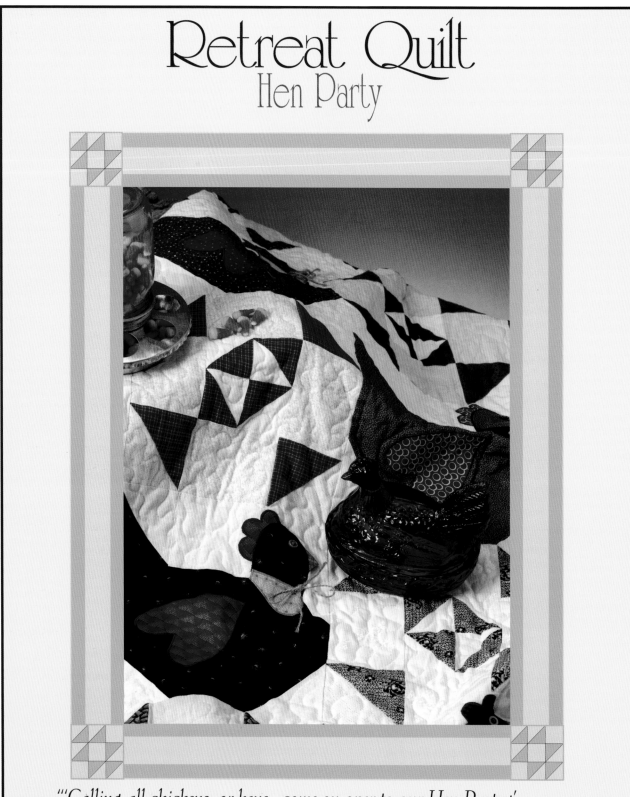

"'Calling all chickens, or hens...come on over to our Hen Party!'
At our Hen Party retreat we cackled, clucked and laughed at all of the
puns we dreamed up to suit our 'corny' theme. The hen house was all
a-flutter that weekend!"

Hen Party

Weather got you cooped-up? Are you all cluckered-out? Sew this "chic" hen quilt with friends while at a Hen Party retreat.

Materials

Finished size is approximately 42" x 50"
Yardage is based on 100 percent cotton fabric that is at least 42" wide.

7 squares 12" x 12" of assorted dark prints for hens' bodies, tails, and heads

7 rectangles 9" x 12" of assorted light prints for hen blocks

7 squares 6" x 6" of assorted red prints for hens' combs and wing appliqués

7 squares 1-1/2" x 1-1/2" of assorted gold prints for hens' beaks

7 rectangles 2" x 3" of assorted prints for hens' collars

7 assorted dark buttons, 3/8" in diameter

8 squares 8" x 8" of assorted dark prints for Barnyard blocks

8 fat eighths (9" x 22") of assorted white-on-white prints for Barnyard blocks

1/3 yard of white-on-white print for inner border

3/4 yard of dark plaid for outer border

1/2 yard of black solid for binding

Batting to fit the finished quilt top

1-3/4 yards of backing, seamed to fit

Cotton twine or yarn (optional)

Cutting Instructions

A 1/4" seam allowance is included in these measurements.

From each of the dark prints for hens, cut:
1 rectangle 7-1/2" x 10-1/2"

1 square 3-1/2" x 3-1/2"

1 of Head template, page 84

From each of the light prints for hens, cut:
1 rectangle 3-1/2" x 10-1/2"

1 square 4-1/2" x 4-1/2"

2 squares 3-1/2" x 3-1/2"

1 square 2-1/2" x 2-1/2"

From each of the assorted red prints for hens, cut:
1 of Comb template

1 of Wing template

From each of the assorted prints for collars, cut:
1 of Collar template

From each dark print for Barnyard blocks, cut:
2 squares 3-7/8" x 3-7/8"; cut these squares in half diagonally to make 4 half-square triangles

2 squares 2-7/8" x 2-7/8"; cut these squares in half diagonally to make 4 half-square triangles

From each white-on-white print fat eighth, cut:
4 rectangles 3-1/2" x 4-1/2"

2 squares 3-7/8" x 3-7/8"; cut these squares in half diagonally to make 4 half-square triangles

2 squares 2-7/8" x 2-7/8"; cut these squares in half diagonally to make 4 half-square triangles

From the white-on-white print for inner border, cut:
2 strips 2-1/2" x 30-1/2"

3 strips 2-1/2" x 42"

From the dark plaid print for outer border, cut:
2 strips 4-1/2" x 34-1/2"

3 strips 4-1/2" x 42"

From the black solid for binding, cut:
5 strips 2-1/2" x 42"

Assembling the Quilt

Piecing the Hen Block

1. Place a light print 4-1/2" square on the lower left-hand corner of the dark print rectangle as shown. With a quilt marker, draw a line from corner to corner. Sew on the drawn line. Press toward the bottom of the rectangle. If desired, trim seam allowance to 1/4".

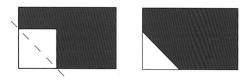

2. In the same manner, sew the light 3-1/2" square to the lower right-hand corner of the dark print rectangle, and sew the light 2-1/2" square to the top right-hand corner.

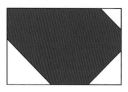

3. In the same manner, sew the dark print 3-1/2" square to the lower left-hand corner of the light print 3-1/2" x 10-1/4" rectangle as shown.

4. Sew the rectangles together as shown.

5. Fold a gold 1-1/2" square diagonally, and then fold it again, forming a prairie point.

6. Position the appliqué pieces on the block as shown. Slip the prairie point under the head, forming a beak. Hand- or machine-appliqué in place (see General Instructions).

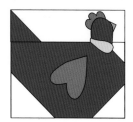

7. Repeat this procedure for the other blocks, making 7 in all. The finished block should measure 10-1/2" including seam allowances.

Piecing the Barnyard Block

1. Sew each dark half-square triangle (the 3-7/8" triangles and the 2-7/8" triangles) to a light one of the same size, making a triangle square. Make a total of 8 triangle squares, 4 of them 2-1/2" x 2-1/2" and 4 of them 3-1/2" x 3-1/2".

2. Arrange the 2-1/2" triangle squares as shown, and sew them together in 2 rows. Sew the rows together to make the center unit.

3. Arrange the light print 3-1/2" x 4-1/2" rectangles, the center unit, and the 3-1/2" triangle squares as shown. Sew them into rows, and then sew the rows together. Make 8 blocks.

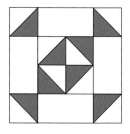

4. Arrange the blocks in 5 rows of 3 blocks each, as shown. Sew them into rows, and then sew the rows together to complete the quilt center.

Adding the Borders

1. Sew a white-on-white 2-1/2" x 30-1/2" strip to the top and bottom of the quilt center. Press seams toward the border.

2. Cut one white-on-white 2-1/2" x 42" strip in half, and sew each half to a full-length strip. Trim them to 54-1/2", and sew them to the sides of the quilt top. Press seams toward the border.

3. Sew a plaid 4-1/2" x 34-1/2" strip to the top and bottom of the quilt center. Press seams toward the border.

4. Cut one plaid 4-1/2" x 42" strip in half, and sew each half to a full-length strip. Trim them to 62-1/2", and sew them to the sides of the quilt center. Press seams toward the border.

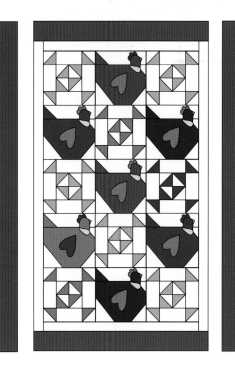

Finishing the Quilt

1. Layer the backing fabric, the batting, and the quilt top.

2. Baste the layers together. Hand- or machine-quilt as desired.

3. Bind the quilt with the solid black 2-1/2"-wide strips (see General Instructions).

4. Sew a button on each hen for an eye, and add a twine or yarn bow to each collar, if desired.

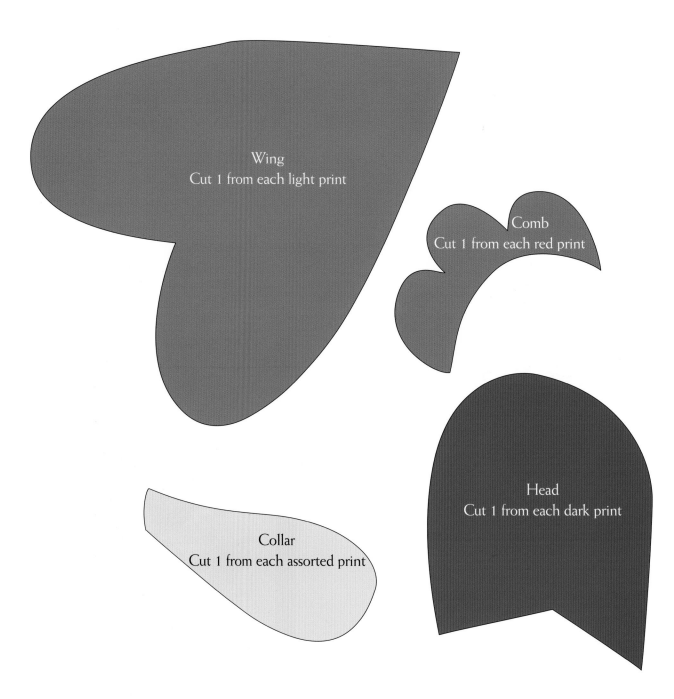

Wing
Cut 1 from each light print

Comb
Cut 1 from each red print

Head
Cut 1 from each dark print

Collar
Cut 1 from each assorted print

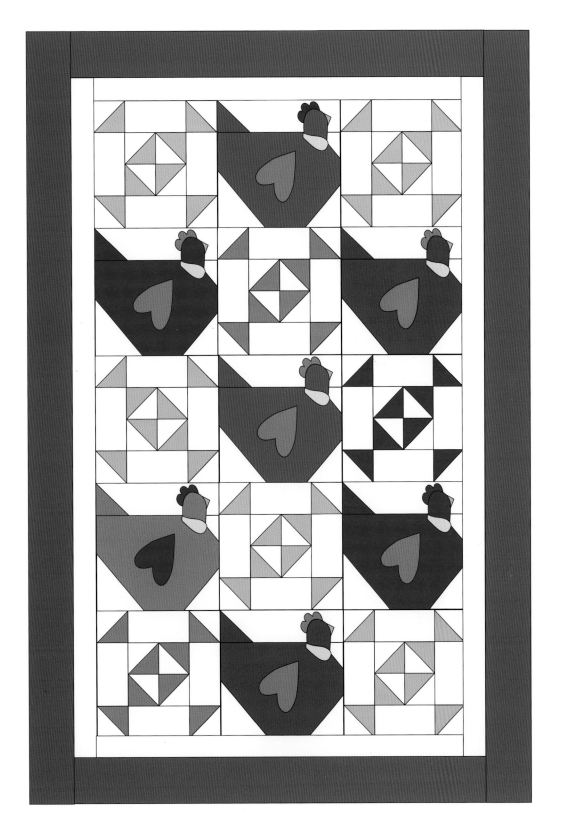

Hen Party Finished Quilt Assembly

Retreat Quilt
Spool Spree

"When I was the Des Moines Area Quilters Guild quilting retreat chair, I made these spool blocks before the retreat and then asked retreat attendees for their signatures. The resulting quilt is a fond remembrance of our time together, spent quilting and having fun."

Spool Spree

Want to unwind and have some fun?
around this signature quilt. Participants c
or use their own scrappy strips to make thi
with signed fabric blocks collected fro

Materials

Finished size is approximately 41" x 41"
Yardage is based on 100 percent cotton fabric that is
at least 42" wide.

8 strips 2-1/2" x 42" of assorted small prints

1 yard of mottled cream for background and inner border

5/8 yard of medium print for outer border

1/3 yard of green solid for binding

15 buttons 1" in diameter (optional)

Batting to fit the finished quilt top

1-1/4 yards of backing

Cutting Instructions

A 1/4" seam allowance is included in these measurements.

From the mottled cream, cut:
   8 strips 2-1/2" x 42"

   2 strips 2-1/2" x 29-1/2"

   2 strips 2-1/2" x 33-1/2"

From the border print, cut:
   2 strips 4" x 33-1/2"

   2 strips 4" x 41-1/2"

From the green solid, cut for binding:
   4 strips 2-1/2" x 42"

Assembling the Quilt

Piecing the Quilt Center

1. Sew a cream 2-1/2" x 42" strip to each of the 8 assorted print 2-1/2" x 42" strips, on the long edges. Press seams toward the print strips.

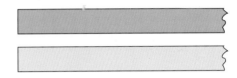

2. Using a quilting ruler that is marked with a 45-degree angle, cut each strip as shown to make 4 triangles with a cream base and 4 triangles with a print base.

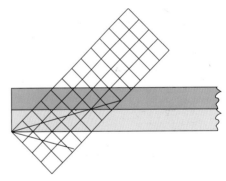

3. For each block, sew 2 cream-base triangles and 2 print-base triangles together as shown. Make 16.

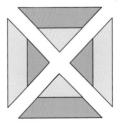

...nge the blocks into 4 rows of 4 blocks each.

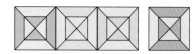

5. Sew the blocks into rows, and sew the rows together.

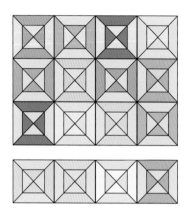

Adding the Borders

1. Sew a cream 2-1/2" x 29-1/2" inner border strip to the top and bottom of the quilt center. Press seams toward the border.

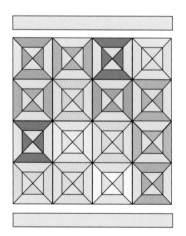

2. Sew a cream 2-1/2" x 33-1/2" inner border strip to each side of the quilt center. Press seams toward the border.

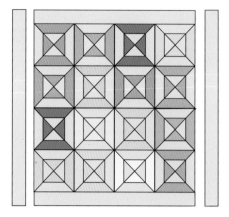

3. Sew a print 4" x 33-1/2" outer border strip to the top and bottom of the quilt center. Press seams toward the border.

4. Sew a print 4" x 41-1/2" outer border strip to each side of the quilt center. Press seams toward the border.

Finishing the Quilt

1. Layer the backing fabric, the batting, and the quilt top.

2. Baste the layers together. Hand- or machine-quilt as desired.

3. Bind the quilt with the green 2-1/2" x 42" strips (see General Instructions).

4. If desired, sew or tie a button to the center of each block.

Spool Spree Finished Quilt Assembly

Milestone Quilts

As your quilting friends make decisions about the quilt pattern, size, and colors, allow your choices to express your emotions. Milestone quilts are made and given away most frequently to express happiness—on the occasion of a baby's birth, a graduation, birthday, wedding or anniversary, moving into a new home, or retirement. A special occasion quilt may also express comfort to those who have lost a loved one, and in the making become a lasting keepsake to grieving family members.

Pattern

A quilt pattern that commemorates an event is more meaningful if your pattern reflects the occasion. Take your cues from these design examples: Hand-prints and foot-prints on a baby's birth quilt; 30 quilt blocks set into a 30th birthday quilt; Double Wedding Ring blocks set into a wedding quilt; 50 star blocks set into a 50th wedding anniversary quilt; signature blocks from co-workers set into a retirement quilt; school and sports T-shirts set into blocks for a high school graduation quilt; photos of quilting friends or a series of signed house blocks set into a quilt for someone who's relocating.

Size and Color

When making a commemorative quilt, out of consideration for the preferences of the recipient it may be prudent to ask what she wants. Not only will you then be able to make your size and color choices based on those preferences, but you'll be able to create something you know the recipient will truly enjoy. An added benefit is that by announcing your intention to make a quilt, you'll also be making a commitment to accomplish it!

Preparing Pieces and Parts

It's important that each person who's making quilt blocks—the block-maker—know exactly what's expected. Here are several possibilities for preparing the pieces and parts for the blocks.

Possibility #1 Provide your block-makers with a block pattern and a sample piece of the fabric that will be used in the quilt border.

If you select a multi-colored border print, block-makers will have several color options when they're choosing fabrics to use in the blocks they sew.

Possiblity #2 Give each block-maker a bag that contains a block pattern and block background fabric. Most often, for the background you'll choose a light value print or solid. Be sure there's enough fabric to sew the required number of blocks, and include extra fabric to allow for accidental cutting mistakes. (Using the same background fabric for every block gives uniformity to the finished quilt.)

Possibility #3 If your quilting friends have decided to make a particular quilt pattern, meet as a group for a "cutting bee" and prepare block bags for distribution to block-makers.

As a group, cut out all the pieces, in all the fabric prints that you'll need to construct the quilt. Stack the cut pieces into individual block piles, then bag them singly for distribution.

Possibility #4 When your group is collecting signatures for a quilt, prepare the signature fabric pieces in advance. Provide each "signer" with two pieces of blank fabric—an extra, in case there's a mistake—that has been backed with freezer paper, and a permanent-ink writing pen. Or your group may decide to ask signers to embroider their names.

To prepare the signature fabric, start by cutting a piece of freezer paper 1/4 inch smaller (on all sides) than the fabric. Center the freezer paper on the fabric back and iron it into place. The freezer paper gives the fabric stability for signing: you can instruct non-quilters to "write only in the area where there's freezer paper on the back." This will ensure that the 1/4" seam allowance is free of writing so that sentiments won't be sewn into the seam allowance. Remove the freezer paper before sewing the signature fabric into a block.

Tips for Making a Special Occasion Quilt

Make a quilt in the recipient's color preferences. If you don't know their preferences, ask someone close to the recipient, or the recipient her/himself.

If it's possible, work into the quilt design the reason for the quilt. For example, 16 hearts for a sweet 16 birthday quilt.

Attach a quilt label to the back of the completed quilt. Note on the label the occasion, date, location, and the quilt maker's name. Add an appropriate sentiment or poem.

Give quilt-care instructions with the quilt, especially if photo-transfers have been used.

Milestone Quilt
Rings of Love

"Weddings and anniversaries are best remembered and commemorated in fabric! The rings of this traditional block represent the never-ending love of a newly-married or long-time-married couple. It's truly an heirloom in the making."

Rings of Love

You can almost hear romance ringing aloud in this lovely pieced quilt bordered by a delicate floral print. Let emotions sing through the work of your hands.

Materials

Finished size is approximately 64" x 76"
Yardage is based on 100 percent cotton fabric that is at least 42" wide.

10 fat quarters of assorted red, yellow, blue, green, and pink solids or small prints for blocks

2-3/4 yards of white solid for blocks and inner border

2 yards of floral print for outer border and binding

Batting to fit the finished quilt top

4 yards of backing, seamed to fit

Cutting Instructions

A 1/4" seam allowance is included in these measurements.

From each fat quarter, cut:

8 squares 3-3/8" x 3-3/8"

8 rectangles 2-1/2" x 4-1/2"

From the white solid, cut:

12 strips 2-7/8" x 42"; from these strips cut 160 squares 2-7/8" x 2-7/8"; cut squares in half diagonally to make 320 half-square triangles

8 strips 4-1/2" x 42"; from these strips cut 80 rectangles 2-1/2" x 4-1/2" and 20 squares 4-1/2" x 4-1/2"

6 strips 2-1/2" x 42" for inner border

From the floral print, cut:

7 strips 6-1/2" x 42" for outer border

8 strips 2-1/2" x 42" for binding

Assembling the Quilt

Piecing the Blocks

1. Sew 2 white half-square triangles to opposite sides of a colored square. Press seams toward the square. Sew half-square triangles to the remaining edges of the colored square to make a square-in-a-square unit. Press seams toward the square. Make a set of 4.

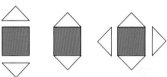

2. Sew a colored 2-1/2" x 4-1/2" rectangle to a white 2-1/2" x 4-1/2" rectangle. Press seam toward the colored rectangle. Make a set of 4.

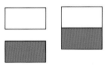

3. Arrange the 4 square-in-a-square units, the 4 rectangle units, and a white square as shown. Sew the units into rows, and sew the rows together to complete a block. Make 4 blocks in each of 5 different colors for a total of 20 blocks.

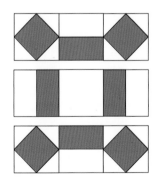

4. Arrange the blocks in 5 rows of 4 blocks each.

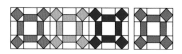

5. Sew the 4 blocks into a row, and sew the 5 rows together to assemble the quilt center.

Adding the Inner Border

1. Cut one 2-1/2" x 42" white strip in half, and sew each half to a full-length strip. Trim them to 48-1/2", and sew them to the top and bottom of the quilt center. Press seams toward the border.

2. Cut another 2-1/2" x 42" white strip in half, and sew each half to a full-length strip. Trim them to 64-1/2", and sew them to the sides of the quilt center.

Adding the Outer Border

1. Cut one floral print 6-1/2" x 42" strip in half, and sew each half to a full-length strip. Trim them to 52-1/2", and sew them to the top and bottom of the quilt center. Press seams toward the border.

2. Sew 2 floral print 6-1/2" x 42" strips together, and trim to 76-1/2". Make 2, and sew them to the sides of the quilt center. Press the seams toward the border.

Finishing the Quilt

1. Layer the backing fabric, the batting, and the quilt top.

2. Baste the layers together. Hand- or machine-quilt as desired.

3. Bind the quilt with the 2-1/2"-wide floral print strips (see General Instructions).

Rings of Love Finished Quilt Assembly

Milestone Quilt
Birthday Bouquet Runner

"Friendship + Food = Celebration! What better time to celebrate friendship than on the occasion of a quilting friend's birthday. These spring-looking blocks sew into a great 'Happy Birthday!' gift. Don't forget the cake and ice cream!"

Birthday Bouquet Runner

Watch a birthday girl's eyes brighten when she sees pieced blocks of colorful fresh flowers sewn and gathered for her by her quilting friends.

Materials

Finished size is approximately 22" x 46"
Yardage is based on 100 percent cotton fabric that is at least 42" wide.

1/2 yard of white solid for background

1/4 yard of mottled yellow print for flower centers and inner border

1/4 yard of mottled pink print for flowers

1/4 yard of mottled lilac print for flowers

3/8 yard of dark green print for leaves

5/8 yard of light green print for leaves and binding

5/8 yard of floral print for outer border

Batting to fit the finished quilt top

1-1/2 yards of backing

Cutting Instructions

A 1/4" seam allowance is included in these measurements.

From the white solid, cut:

12 squares 1-1/2" x 1-1/2"

12 rectangles 1-1/2" x 2-1/2"

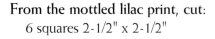

12 squares 2-7/8" x 2-7/8"; cut these squares in half diagonally to make 24 half-square triangles

From the mottled yellow print, cut:

12 squares 1-1/2" x 1-1/2"

2 strips 1-1/2" x 12-1/2"

2 strips 1-1/2" x 38-1/2"

From the mottled pink print, cut:

6 squares 2-1/2" x 2-1/2"

3 squares 2-7/8" x 2-7/8"; cut these squares in half diagonally to make 6 half-square triangles

From the mottled lilac print, cut:

6 squares 2-1/2" x 2-1/2"

3 squares 2-7/8" x 2-7/8"; cut these squares in half diagonally to make 6 half-square triangles

From the light green print, cut:

6 squares 2-1/2" x 2-1/2"

12 squares 2-7/8" x 2-7/8"; cut these squares in half diagonally to make 24 half-square triangles

4 strips 2-1/2" x 42"

From the dark green print, cut:

6 squares 2-1/2" x 2-1/2"

12 squares 2-7/8" x 2-7/8"; cut these squares in half diagonally to make 24 half-square triangles

From the floral print, cut:

2 strips 4-1/2" x 14-1/2"

3 strips 4-1/2" x 42"

Piecing the Blocks

1. Make 12 blocks. Half will have pink, half purple; half will have light green, half dark green.

2. Sew a light or dark green half-square triangle to a white half-square triangle to make a leaf triangle square. Press seam toward the green. Make 4.

3. Sew a pink or lilac half-square triangle to a white half-square triangle to make a petal triangle square. Press seam toward the pink or lilac. Make 2.

4. Sew the yellow square to the white square. Press seam toward the yellow. Sew the unit to the white rectangle to make a flower center.

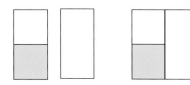

5. Arrange a green square, the leaf units, the pink or lilac square, the petal units, and the flower center as shown. Sew the pieces into rows, and then sew the rows together.

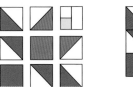

Assembling the Runner

1. Arrange the 12 completed blocks in 6 rows of 2 blocks as shown. Sew the blocks into rows, and sew the rows together.

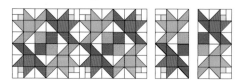

2. Sew a 1-1/2" x 12-1/2" yellow inner border strip to each end of the runner. Press seams toward the border.

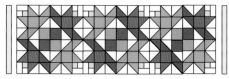

3. Sew a 1-1/2" x 38-1/2" yellow inner border strip to each side of the runner. Press seams toward the border.

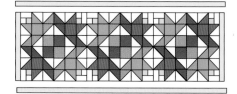

4. Sew 4-1/2" x 14-1/2" floral print outer border strips to the ends of the runner. Press seams toward the border.

5. Cut one floral print outer border strip in half, and sew each half to a full-length strip. Trim the strips to 46-1/2", and sew one to each side of the runner. Press seams toward the border.

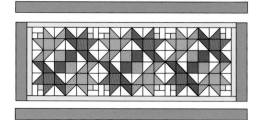

Finishing the Runner

1. Layer the backing fabric, the batting, and the runner.

2. Baste the layers together. Hand- or machine-quilt as desired.

3. Bind the runner with the 2-1/2"-wide light green strips (see General Instructions).

Birthday Bouquet Finished Quilt Assembly

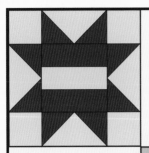

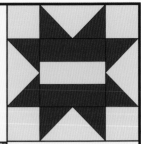

Everybody in my quilting group has different ideas, so when we bounce them off each other, I become more creative. The talking and eating are great too!

—Christy Drake

Quilting friends do more than get together and quilt. We're there for each other during life's ups and downs. Support and encouragement are really what our relationships are all about.

—Lynn Johnson

When quilting friends spend time together, friendships form quickly and it feels right to make quilts for each other— when babies are born, a divorce happens, someone moves, a family member dies, or someone is recovering from surgery. It feels wonderful to curl up with a quilt that's just been made especially for you by special friends.

—Julie Armstrong

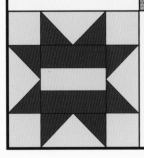

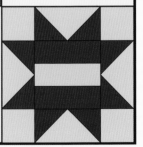

I've given away nearly all the quilts I've ever made, but the quilts I've made with my friends are the ones I'll keep forever—that's how much my quilting friends mean to me.

—Carmen Clark

Sharing Blocks

SHARING BLOCKS

You'll find plenty of inspiring ideas in the following pages. Our gallery of finished quilts will lead to more ideas your quilting friends can try, and the more than fifty block patterns, offered in multiple size options, are our favorites to share with you.

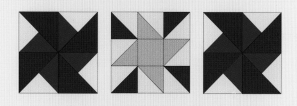

Fabric Exchange Gallery

Block Swap Gallery

Block Shower Gallery

Row Quilt Gallery

Round Robin Gallery

Charity and Children Gallery

Milestones Gallery

Retreats Gallery

Blocks to Share

Fabric Exchange Gallery

Ladies

As a group, choose a quilt pattern everyone wants to make. Then swap enough prints to sew the quilt. Decide whether you want to trade 1/4 yard, 1/3 yard, or 1/2 yard cuts. For these quilts, friends swapped blue fabric prints to make the same pattern. Then they individualized each quilt by selecting their own background color preference: white, yellow, or light blue.

(L-R): Cindy Ohmart, Diane Crawford, Jill Reber

Blue Fabric

Fat quarters (18" x 22") are readily available in quilt shops and fabric stores, and the size offers many options for cutting and sewing into quilt blocks. Try this: select one print, purchase 2 yards, cut it into fat quarters, keep one and swap the rest with seven other friends. It's also simple to cut fabric into 2" strips, as these quilters did. Then choose a pattern to make from the variety of fabrics you collect.

(L-R): Jill Reber, Anne Henter, Jill Reber

Countless quilt blocks and designs are possible with fabrics collected in a color-oriented or themed-print fabric swap. Whether you choose from the ideas here or head off in a new direction, a fabric exchange is a wonderful opportunity to add more color and design to your fabric inventory.

Autumn

Try swapping fabric that has been cut into specific-size pieces. Select a block design or pattern first; then cut appropriate-sized pieces. Or, choose an acrylic template from which to cut fabric shapes. Here, quilters swapped 6" squares and 3" x 12" rectangles of fall-colored and printed fabrics.

(L-R) Jill Reber, Jill Reber, Cindy Ohmart

Amish

A solid-color swap is a great way to collect fabrics for an Amish-style quilt, or simply to add variety to your fabric inventory. Whether you exchange 1/3 yard cuts or 3" strips, block designs sewn with assorted solid colors and black seem Amish.

(L) Cindy Ohmart, (R) Jill Reber, (Top) Anne Henter

Block Swap Gallery

6-Inch Blocks

An easy-to-organize block swap is one that's based only on size and color. Choose to make 4", 6", 8", 10", 12" or 14" blocks, agree on a color scheme, and decide how many blocks each quilter should make every month. Allow participants to choose different block designs so you'll collect an interesting variety. The quilts shown were made with 6" blocks sewn from dark country prints and tan backgrounds. Each quilter sewed four blocks each month for 12 months.

(L) Cindy Ohmart, (R) Jill Reber

30's Prints

Organize a themed block swap where your quilting friends trade reproduction fabrics (1930s, Civil War), batiks, homespuns, children's prints, sports prints, or leaf prints. Make all blocks the same design and size. These quilters purchased a bolt of white fabric for use in the background of every 6" (finished) block.

(L Ladder Top) Carmen Clark, (L Ladder Bottom) Cindy Ohmart, (R Ladder Top) Jill Reber, (R Ladder Bottom) Deanne Main, (L Lower) Christy Drake, (Middle) Diane Crawford, (R) Anne Henter

Take the idea of swapping one step further than a fabric swap. Sew blocks to exchange with your quilting friends. These block swap quilts will help launch your inspiration to create your own one-of-a-kind quilt with your quilting friends.

Patriotic Lottery

Take a chance at becoming a lucky-blocks winner! Ask quilters to make a block in a particular size, design and color scheme. Then put names into a hat and draw a winner. If a quilter makes two, three, or four blocks, she has two, three, or four chances to win. Quilts shown here are sewn with star blocks made from red, white, and blue prints

(L) Jill Reber, (Top) Jill Reber, (R) Peggy Warner

Calendar

Try making a calendar quilt with 12 quilting friends. You'll each make a block representative of a month, and make it 12 times. Or organize six friends to make two calendar blocks. Appliquéd motifs are best suited for representing a particular month, and can be the center of a pieced block. For fun, ask each quilting friend to draw her month from a hat. For these quilts, motifs have been machine-appliquéd onto 12" (finished) Cypress blocks.

(Left Cupboard Door) Carmen Clark,
(Right Cupboard Door) Deanne Main,
(Inside Cupboard Top Shelf) Jill Reber,
(Inside Cupboard Middle Shelf) Cindy Ohmart,
(Inside Cupboard Bottom Shelf) Diane Crawford

Block Shower Gallery

Each quilt in this gallery was made from blocks "showered" on one quilter within a group of quilting friends. As in a block swap, a multitude of options for block-making are available, and every resulting finished quilt is lovely and unique.

Country Colors

Say thank you to a guild president or other group leader, or surprise a quilting friend on a special occasion with a stack of matching blocks. The center quilt shown is the result of a surprise shower of 52 Card Trick blocks (see page 119) given on the occasion of a 52nd birthday.

Colors (Left Top) Carmen Clark, (Top) Jill Reber, (Middle) Cindy Ohmart, (Right Bottom) Deanne Main

Soft Pastels

Over the course of a year allow each quilter in your group to be showered with blocks in her favorite color scheme or themed print, size and design. For consistency, she may provide some of the fabric to be used. Here, each quilter requested "soft pastel" blocks and provided the background fabric for block-piecing or appliqué.

(Top) Jill Reber, (Bottom) Anne Henter

Block Shower Green

Instead of shopping for birthday gifts for quilting friends, ask each quilter to choose a block design and colors she'd like to receive during her birthday month. These quilters chose different blocks, but the same green and cream color schemes

(L) Lynn Johnson (R) Jill Reber

Row Quilt Gallery

A row quilt allows each participant's personality and creativity to shine. The finished quilts reflect the owner's tastes and preferences in fabric and design. Let these row quilts inspire you to get to know your quilting friends even better.

Row Quilts Group 1

Ask each quilter in your group to choose a theme for her row quilt. Adopt themes from gardening, seasons, farming, animals, children, hobbies, foods, or personalities. Quilts here are expressions of Iowa, mountains, and lake themes. As one row quilt owner did, take your inspiration from a border print fabric

Photo One (L) Lynn Johnson, (M) Julie Armstrong, (R) Jill Reber

Row Quilts Group 2

When organizing a row quilt exchange, as a group, make a decision about size. Then, individually make key decisions about themes and color schemes. Document everything as 'rules' to include in a special "pass box" that travels to each row quilter. Also place in the box one or two pieces of fabric and the row quilt owner's journal.

Photo Two (L) Diane Crawford, (M) Jill Reber, (R) Deanne Main

Round Robin Gallery

This gallery will motivate you to organize a round robin exchange among your quilting friends. It's thoroughly delightful to watch a quilt "grow" round-by-round, knowing that it includes the best talents of your quilting friends.

Row Quilts Group 3

Decide what size your row quilts will be. A common row width is 60" that can be finished without adding a border. Or consider adding borders to rows that have been sewn 42" to 45" wide. Choose a bolt width because it will not need to be pieced for appliqué work. More ideas for row quilt themes include: "My Garden," "Baskets," and "My Favorite Things."

Photo Three (L) Cindy Ohmart, (L Middle) Carmen Clark, (R Middle) Diane Crawford, (R) Peggy Warner

Round Robin

Quilting friends who have successfully made row quilts should consider organizing a round robin. To get started, agree on rules about size, colors, and techniques for each round or pass. Choose colors and techniques for each round that will enhance the owner's center block. Here, four quilts shown reflect a rule that the center square be placed on point.

(Clockwise from L) Jody Hamlin,
Char Rathbone, Marcia Jacobs, Jeanne Stilley,
Char Rathbone

Charity & Children Gallery

Choose a color scheme and swap enough fabrics so you and your friends can make the same quilt pattern. Personalize your quilt by choosing your own background fabric as these quilters did using white. Brights or pastels were then added.

Baby Brights
Quilters' children whose baby quilts are shown include:
Mitchell, Ellie and Tyler Crawford
Jessica and Michael Henter
Cooper Johnson

Retreats Gallery

Whether two quilters or a dozen get together to organize a themed retreat, planning is fun! Loosen your creativity to incorporate your theme into all aspects of your retreat—invitations, table centerpieces, favors, door prizes, food, beverages—and even personalized wastebaskets for every quilter. When the creativity of a retreat group starts flowing, imaginative quilts grow from identical blocks. Each of these six chicken quilts was hatched from the same fifteen blocks.

Hen Party
(Upper L) Deanne Main, (Lower L) Diane Crawford, (Top Middle) Lynn Johnson, (Bottom Middle) Jill Reber, (Upper R) Cindy Ohmart, (Lower R) Carmen Clark

Milestones Gallery

Photo Transfer

Secretly select black and white or color photographs, transfer them onto fabric, and make a surprise quilt commemorating a special occasion. For this 25th anniversary quilt, under false pretenses friends acquired photos, transferred them onto plain fabric and set the fabric into Sawtooth Star blocks.

Jill and Jim Reber's 25th anniversary quilt.

Weddings & Anniversaries

Try this. Choose one print fabric to be used as a quilt border. Give a block pattern to your friends, asking them to make blocks in colors that coordinate with the border fabric. Or, give the same background fabric to all your friends, inviting them to make blocks in a particular color scheme

(Top) Jill Reber's 20th Anniversary quilt,
(R) Deanne and Matt Main's 15th Anniversary quilt
(L) Fran and Cal Wiseman's 50th Anniversary quilt

Each quilt shown here marks a special occasion—when quilters organized to commemorate an event. Take your cues from the works of these quilting friends to honor someone special within or outside of your group.

Signature Quilts

Make a signature quilt to remember a special event such as a graduation or a going-away. Pre-planning is needed. Cut plain fabric pieces that are larger than what will be used in the finished block. So guests can sign the plain fabric, stabilize it with freezer paper ironed to the fabric back. Provide a permanent-ink pen, or have guests sign in pencil so signatures can later be embroidered. Remove the freezer paper before sewing the signatures into quilt blocks.

(L) Matt Reber's High School Graduation quilt
(M) Lynn Johnson's Moving Away quilt,
(R) Jill Reber's Thank You quilt
(Middle Bottom) Jill Reber's Quilting Class Remembrance quilt

Graduation

For a graduation quilt, select a themed fabric that reflects the recipient's personality, or choose the school's colors. Try sewing a quilt from some of the T-shirts collected from special activities or events.

(L) Carmen Clark's College Graduation quilt,
(Left Middle) John Warner's High School Graduation quilt,
(Top) Dawn Warner's High School Graduation quilt,
(R) Dawn Warner's High School Graduation quilt

Blocks to Share

It's a block bonanza that's meant to be shared! The block designs and numerous size options on the following pages offer you and your quilting friends countless swapping possibilities—for your next block exchange or block shower, or row quilt or round robin exchange.

Album Star

Color	Shape	6"	9"	12"	15"
Cream	A-4 squares	2"	2-3/4"	3-1/2"	4-1/4"
	C-4 q/s triangles	4-1/4"	5-3/4"	7-1/4"	8-3/4"
	D-1 rectangle	1-1/2" x 3-1/2"	2" x 5"	2-1/2" x 6-1/2"	3" x 8"
Brown	B-8 h/s triangles	2-3/8"	3-1/8"	3-7/8"	4-5/8"
	D-2 rectangles	1-1/2" x 3-1/2"	2" x 5"	2-1/2" x 6-1/2"	3" x 8"

Angela's Star

Color	Shape	6"	8"	10"	12"
Cream	A-4 squares	2"	2-1/2"	3"	3-1/2"
	B-8 h/s triangles	2-3/8"	2-7/8"	3-3/8"	3-7/8"
Blue	A-2 squares	2"	2-1/2"	3"	3-1/2"
	B-4 h/s triangles	2-3/8"	2-7/8"	3-3/8"	3-7/8"
Red	A-2 squares	2"	2-1/2"	3"	3-1/2"
	B-4 h/s triangles	2-3/8"	2-7/8"	3-3/8"	3-7/8"

Antique Tiles

Color	Shape	6"	9"	12"	15"
Cream	B-4 rectangles	1-1/2" x 2-1/2"	2" x 3-1/2"	2-1/2" x 4-1/2"	3" x 5-1/2"
Lt. Pink	A-1 square	2-1/2"	3-1/2"	4-1/2"	5-1/2"
	B-4 rectangles	1-1/2" x 2-1/2"	2" x 3-1/2"	2-1/2" x 4-1/2"	3" x 5-1/2"
	C-4 squares	1-1/2"	2"	2-1/2"	3"
Dk. Pink	B-4 rectangles	1-1/2" x 2-1/2"	2" x 3-1/2"	2-1/2" x 4-1/2"	3" x 5-1/2"
	C-4 squares	1-1/2"	2"	2-1/2"	3"

See page 132 for h/s and q/s cutting instructions

Sharing Blocks

Baby Basket

Color	Shape	6"	8"	10"	12"
Cream	A-1 h/s triangle	3-7/8"	4-7/8"	5-7/8"	6-7/8"
	C-2 rectangles	2" x 3-1/2"	2-1/2" x 4-1/2"	3" x 5-1/2"	3-1/2" x 6-1/2"
	D-1 square	2"	2-1/2"	3"	3-1/2"
	E-2 q/s triangles	4-1/4"	5-1/4"	6-1/4"	7-1/4"
Blue	B-6 h/s triangles	2-3/8"	2-7/8"	3-3/8"	3-7/8"
	D-2 squares	2"	2-1/2"	3"	3-1/2"
Yellow	D-2 squares	2"	2-1/2"	3"	3-1/2"

Basic Four Patch

Color	Shape	4"	6"	8"	9"
Dk. Green	A-2 squares	2-1/2"	3-1/2"	4-1/2"	5"
Lt. Green	A-2 squares	2-1/2"	3-1/2"	4-1/2"	5"

Bear Paw

Color	Shape	7"	10-1/2"	14"	21"
White Print	A-4 rectangles	1-1/2" x 3-1/2"	2" x 5"	2-1/2" x 6-1/2"	3-1/2" x 9-1/2"
	C-4 squares	1-1/2"	2"	2-1/2"	3-1/2"
	D-16 h/s triangles	1-7/8"	2-3/8"	2-7/8"	3-7/8"
Red	B-4 squares	2-1/2"	3-1/2"	4-1/2"	6-1/2"
Blue	C-1 square	1-1/2"	2"	2-1/2"	3-1/2"
	D-16 h/s triangles	1-7/8"	2-3/8"	2-7/8"	3-7/8"

See page 132 for h/s and q/s cutting instructions

Sharing Blocks

Best Friends

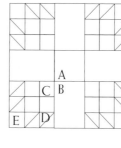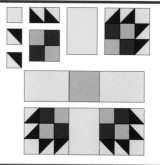

Color	Shape	8"	14"	16"	24"
Cream	B-4 rectangles	2-1/2" x 3-1/2"	4" x 5-3/4"	4-1/2" x 6-1/2"	6-1/2" x 9-1/2"
	D-16 h/s triangles	1-7/8"	2-5/8"	2-7/8"	3-7/8"
	E-4 squares	1-1/2"	2-1/4"	2-1/2"	3-1/2"
Lt. Blue	A-1 square	2-1/2"	4"	4-1/2"	6-1/2"
	C-8 squares	1-1/2"	2-1/4"	2-1/2"	3-1/2"
Med. Blue	A-8 squares	1-1/2"	2-1/4"	2-1/2"	3-1/2"
Dk. Blue	D-16 h/s triangles	1-7/8"	2-5/8"	2-7/8"	3-7/8"

Big T

Color	Shape	6"	9"	12"	15"
Cream	A-4 h/s triangles	2-7/8"	3-7/8"	4-7/8"	5-7/8"
	B-4 q/s triangles	3-1/4"	4-1/4"	5-1/4"	6-1/4"
Lt. Blue	D-4 rectangles	1-1/2" x 2-1/2"	2" x 3-1/2"	2-1/2" x 4-1/2"	3" x 5-1/2"
Dk. Blue	C-8 h/s triangles	1-7/8"	2-3/8"	2-7/8"	3-3/8"
Red	A-4 h/s triangles	2-7/8"	3-7/8"	4-7/8"	5-7/8"
	E-1 square	2-1/2"	3-1/2"	4-1/2"	5-1/2"

Birds In The Air

Color	Shape	6"	9"	12"	15"
Cream	A-1 h/s triangles	6-7/8"	9-7/8"	12-7/8"	15-7/8"
	B-3 h/s triangles	2-7/8"	3-7/8"	4-7/8"	5-7/8"
Blue	B-6 h/s triangles	2-7/8"	3-7/8"	4-7/8"	5-7/8"

See page 132 for h/s and q/s cutting instructions

Sharing Blocks

Blocks in a Row

Color	Shape	3"	6"	9"	12"
Cream	A-1 square	1-1/2"	2-1/2"	3-1/2"	4-1/2"
Green	A-2 squares	1-1/2"	2-1/2"	3-1/2"	4-1/2"
	B-2 rectangles	1-1/2" x 3-1/2"	2-1/2" x 6-1/2"	3-1/2" x 9-1/2"	4-1/2" x 12-1/2"

Broken Dishes

Color	Shape	4"	6"	8"	10"	12"
Cream	4-A h/s triangles	2-7/8"	3-7/8"	4-7/8"	5-7/8"	6-7/8"
Pink	4-A h/s triangles	2-7/8"	3-7/8"	4-7/8"	5-7/8"	6-7/8"

Cake Stand Basket

Color	Shape	6"	8"	10"	12"
Cream	A-1 square	2"	2-1/2"	3"	3-1/2"
	B-4 h/s triangles	2-3/8"	2-7/8"	3-3/8"	3-7/8"
	C-2 h/s triangles	3-7/8"	4-7/8"	5-7/8"	6-7/8"
	D-2 rectangles	2" x 3-1/2"	2-1/2" x 4-1/2"	3" x 5-1/2"	3-1/2" x 6-1/2"
Purple	B-4 h/s triangles	2-3/8"	2-7/8"	3-3/8"	3-7/8"
	C-1 h/s triangle	3-7/8"	4-7/8"	5-7/8"	6-7/8"

See page 132 for h/s and q/s cutting instructions

Sharing Blocks

Calico Puzzle

Color	Shape	3"	6"	9"	12"
Cream	B-4 h/s triangles	1-7/8"	2-7/8"	3-7/8"	4-7/8"
Gold	A-1 square	1-1/2"	2-1/2"	3-1/2"	4-1/2"
	B-4 h/s triangles	1-7/8"	2-7/8"	3-7/8"	4-7/8"
Green	A-4 squares	1-1/2"	2-1/2"	3-1/2"	4-1/2"

Card Trick

Color	Shape	6"	9"	12"	15"
Cream	A-4 h/s triangles	2-7/8"	3-7/8"	4-7/8"	5-7/8"
	B-4 q/s triangles	3-1/4"	4-1/4"	5-1/4"	6-1/4"
Black	A-2 h/s triangles	2-7/8"	3-7/8"	4-7/8"	5-7/8"
	B-2 q/s triangles	3-1/4"	4-1/4"	5-1/4"	6-1/4"
Blue	A-2 h/s triangles	2-7/8"	3-7/8"	4-7/8"	5-7/8"
	B-2 q/s triangles	3-1/4"	4-1/4"	5-1/4"	6-1/4"
Red	A-2 h/s triangles	2-7/8"	3-7/8"	4-7/8"	5-7/8"
	B-2 q/s triangles	3-1/4"	4-1/4"	5-1/4"	6-1/4"
Purple	A-2 h/s triangles	2-7/8"	3-7/8"	4-7/8"	5-7/8"
	B-2 q/s triangles	3-1/4"	4-1/4"	5-1/4"	6-1/4"

Churn Dash

Color	Shape	5"	7-1/2"	10"	15"
Grey	A-4 h/s triangles	2-7/8"	3-7/8"	4-7/8"	6-7/8"
	B-5 squares	1-1/2"	2"	2-1/2"	3-1/2"
Black	A-4 h/s triangles	2-7/8"	3-7/8"	4-7/8"	6-7/8"
	B-4 squares	1-1/2"	2"	2-1/2"	3-1/2"

Clay's Choice

Color	Shape	6"	8"	10"	12"
Cream	A-4 squares	2"	2-1/2"	3"	3-1/2"
	B-4 h/s triangles	2-3/8"	2-7/8"	3-5/8"	3-7/8"
Red	A-4 squares	2"	2-1/2"	3"	3-1/2"
	B-4 h/s triangles	2-3/8"	2-7/8"	3-5/8"	3-7/8"
Blue	B-8 h/s triangles	2-3/8"	2-7/8"	3-5/8"	3-7/8"

Country Lanes

Color	Shape	5"	7-1/2"	10"	15"
Cream	B-4 rectangles	1-1/2" x 2-1/2"	2" x 3-1/2"	2-1/2" x 4-1/2"	3-1/2" x 6-1/2"
Black	A-9 squares	1-1/2"	2"	2-1/2"	3-1/2"
Brown	A-8 squares	1-1/2"	2"	2-1/2"	3-1/2"

Cracker

Color	Shape	6"	8"	9"	10"	12"
Cream	A-2 h/s triangles	3-7/8"	4-7/8"	5-3/8"	5-7/8"	6-7/8"
	B-1 rectangle	2" x 4-3/4"	2-3/8" x 6-1/8"	2-5/8" x 6-7/8"	2-7/8" x 7-5/8"	3-3/8" x 9"
Red	A-2 h/s triangles	3-7/8"	4-7/8"	5-3/8"	5-7/8"	6-7/8"
	B-2 rectangles	2" x 4-3/4"	2-3/8" x 6-1/8"	2-5/8" x 6-7/8"	2-7/8" x 7-5/8"	3-3/8" x 9"

See page 132 for h/s and q/s cutting instructions

Sharing Blocks

Cypress

Color	Shape	6"	8"	10"	12"
Cream	A-12 h/s triangles	2-3/8"	2-7/8"	3-3/8"	3-7/8"
	C-1 square	3-1/2"	4-1/2"	5-1/2"	6-1/2"
Lt. Blue	A-4 h/s triangles	2-3/8"	2-7/8"	3-3/8"	3-7/8"
Dk. Blue	B-4 q/s triangles	4-1/4"	5-1/4"	6-1/4"	7-1/4"

Double Pinwheel

Color	Shape	6"	8"	10"	12"
Blue	A-4 h/s triangles	3-7/8"	4-7/8"	5-7/8"	6-7/8"
Red	B-4 q/s triangles	4-1/4"	5-1/4"	6-1/4"	7-1/4"
Tan	B-4 q/s triangles	4-1/4"	5-1/4"	6-1/4"	7-1/4"

Dutchman's Puzzle

Color	Shape	6"	8"	10"	12"
Cream	B-16 h/s triangles	2-3/8"	2-7/8"	3-3/8"	3-7/8"
Gold	A-4 q/s triangles	4-1/4"	5-1/4"	6-1/4"	7-1/4"
Blue	A-4 q/s triangles	4-1/4"	5-1/4"	6-1/4"	7-1/4"

See page 132 for h/s and q/s cutting instructions

Sharing Blocks

Eccentric Star

Color	Shape	3"	6"	9"	12"
Cream	B-8 h/s triangles	1-7/8"	2-7/8"	3-7/8"	4-7/8"
Lt. Blue	B-4 h/s triangles	1-7/8"	2-7/8"	3-7/8"	4-7/8"
	A-1 square	1-1/2"	2-1/2"	3-1/2"	4-1/2"
Dk. Blue	B-4 h/s triangles	1-7/8"	2-7/8"	3-7/8"	4-7/8"

English Wedding Ring

Color	Shape	5"	7-1/2"	10"	15"
Tan	A-5 squares	1-1/2"	2"	2-1/2"	3-1/2"
	B-16 h/s triangles	1-7/8"	2-3/8"	2-7/8"	3-7/8"
Red	A-4 squares	1-1/2"	2"	2-1/2"	3-1/2"
	B-16 h/s triangles	1-7/8"	2-3/8"	2-7/8"	3-7/8"

Flying Geese

Color	Shape	5"	7-1/2"	10"	12-1/2"
Cream	B-18 h/s triangles	1-7/8"	2-3/8"	2-7/8"	3-3/8"
Brown	A-4 q/s triangles	3-1/4"	4-1/4"	5-1/4"	6-1/4"
	C-1 square	1-1/2"	2"	2-1/2"	3"
Peach	A-4 q/s triangles	3-1/4"	4-1/4"	5-1/4"	6-1/4"
Gold	A-4 q/s triangles	3-1/4"	4-1/4"	5-1/4"	6-1/4"

See page 132 for h/s and q/s cutting instructions

Sharing Blocks

Four Square

Color	Shape	6"	9"	12"	15"
Cream	B-8 squares	1-1/2"	2"	2-1/2"	3"
Rust	A-4 squares	2-1/2"	3-1/2"	4-1/2"	5-1/2"
Blue	A-8 squares	1-1/2"	2"	2-1/2"	3"

Fox and Geese

Color	Shape	6"	8"	10"	12"
Cream	A-10 h/s triangles	2-3/8"	2-7/8"	3-3/8"	3-7/8"
Black	A-2 h/s triangles	3-7/8"	4-7/8"	5-7/8"	6-7/8"
	C-2 h/s triangles	2-3/8"	2-7/8"	3-3/8"	3-7/8"
Brown	A-2 h/s triangles	2-3/8"	2-7/8"	3-3/8"	3-7/8"
Peach	B-2 squares	2"	2-1/2"	3"	3-1/2"

Hands of Friendship

Color	Shape	6"	9"	12"	15"
Cream	A-4 squares	2-1/2"	3-1/2"	4-1/2"	5-1/2"
	C-4 q/s triangles	3-1/4"	4-1/4"	5-1/4"	6-1/4"
Purple	B-2 q/s triangles	4"	5-1/2"	7"	8-3/8"
	C-4 q/s triangles	3-1/4"	4-1/4"	5-1/4"	6-1/4"
Pink	B-2 q/s triangles	4"	5-1/2"	7"	8-3/8"
	C-4 q/s triangles	3-1/4"	4-1/4"	5-1/4"	6-1/4"

See page 132 for h/s and q/s cutting instructions

Sharing Blocks

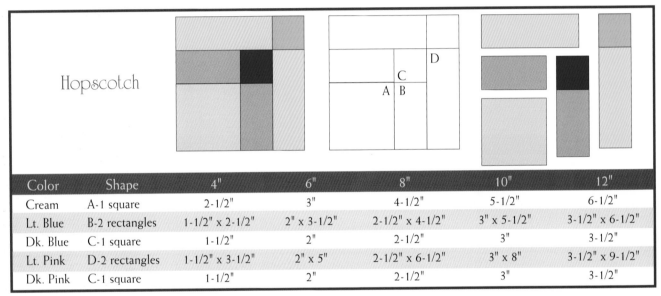

Hen & Chicks

Color	Shape	5"	7-1/2"	10"	15"
Cream	B-4 rectangles	1-1/2" x 2-1/2"	2" x 3-1/2"	2-1/2" x 5-1/2"	3-1/2" x 6-1/2"
	C-12 h/s triangles	1-7/8"	2-3/8"	2-7/8"	3-7/8"
Blue	A-4 h/s triangles	2-7/8"	3-7/8"	4-7/8"	6-7/8"
	C-4 h/s triangles	1-7/8"	2-3/8"	2-7/8"	3-7/8"
	D-1 square	1-1/2"	2"	2-1/2"	3-1/2"

Hopscotch

Color	Shape	4"	6"	8"	10"	12"
Cream	A-1 square	2-1/2"	3"	4-1/2"	5-1/2"	6-1/2"
Lt. Blue	B-2 rectangles	1-1/2" x 2-1/2"	2" x 3-1/2"	2-1/2" x 4-1/2"	3" x 5-1/2"	3-1/2" x 6-1/2"
Dk. Blue	C-1 square	1-1/2"	2"	2-1/2"	3"	3-1/2"
Lt. Pink	D-2 rectangles	1-1/2" x 3-1/2"	2" x 5"	2-1/2" x 6-1/2"	3" x 8"	3-1/2" x 9-1/2"
Dk. Pink	C-1 square	1-1/2"	2"	2-1/2"	3"	3-1/2"

Indian

Color	Shape	6"	8"	10"	12"
Cream	C-1 square	3-1/2"	4-1/2"	5-1/2"	6-1/2"
Brown	B-8 h/s triangles	2-3/8"	2-7/8"	3-3/8"	3-7/8"
	A-2 squares	2"	2-1/2"	3"	3-1/2"
Orange	B-8 h/s triangles	2-3/8"	2-7/8"	3-3/8"	3-7/8"
	A-2 squares	2"	2-1/2"	3"	3-1/2"

See page 132 for h/s and q/s cutting instructions

Sharing Blocks

King's Crown

Color	Shape	6"	8"	10"	12"
Cream	A-8 h/s triangles	2-3/8"	2-7/8"	3-3/8"	3-7/8"
	C-1 square	3-1/2"	4-1/2"	5-1/2"	6-1/2"
Lt. Green	B-4 q/s triangles	4-1/4"	5-1/4"	6-1/4"	7-1/4"
Dk. Green	D-4 squares	2"	2-1/2"	3"	3-1/2"

London Roads

Color	Shape	9"	13-1/2"	18"
Cream	A-4 h/s triangles	3-7/8"	5-3/8"	6-7/8"
	D-1 square	3-1/2"	4"	6-1/2"
Gold	B-4 q/s triangles	4-1/4"	5-3/4"	7-1/4"
	C-4 rectangles	1-1/2" x 3-1/2"	2" x 5"	2-1/2" x 6-1/2"
Lt. Green	B-4 q/s triangles	4-1/4"	5-3/4"	7-1/4"
	C-4 rectangles	1-1/2" x 3-1/2"	2" x 5"	2-1/2" x 6-1/2"
Dk. Green	B-4 q/s triangles	4-1/4"	5-3/4"	7-1/4"
	C-4 rectangles	1-1/2" x 3-1/2"	2" x 5"	2-1/2" x 6-1/2"

Louisiana Pinwheel

Color	Shape	6"	8"	10"	12"
Tan	A-4 rectangles	2" x 3-1/2"	2-1/2" x 4-1/2"	3" x 5-1/2"	3-1/2" x 6-1/2"
Lt. Blue	B-8 h/s triangles	2-3/8"	2-7/8"	3-3/8"	3-7/8"
Dk. Blue	C-4 q/s triangles	4-1/4"	5-1/4"	6-1/4"	7-1/4"

See page 132 for h/s and q/s cutting instructions

Sharing Blocks

Maple Leaf

Color	Shape	6"	9"	12"	15"
Cream	A-1 square	2-1/2"	3-1/2"	4-1/2"	5-1/2"
	B-4 h/s triangles	2-7/8"	3-7/8"	4-7/8"	5-7/8"
	D-2 h/s triangles	2-5/8"	3-5/8"	4-5/8"	5-5/8"
Brown	A-1 square	2-1/2"	3-1/2"	4-1/2"	5-1/2"
	B-4 h/s triangles	2-7/8"	3-7/8"	4-7/8"	5-7/8"
	C-1 rectangle	2-1/2" x 4-1/2"	3-1/2" x 6-1/2"	4-1/2" x 8-1/2"	5-1/2" x 10-1/2"
	E-1 rectangle	1" x 3"	1" x 4-1/2"	1" x 6"	1" x 7-1/2"

Note: Trim off stem rectangle after attaching D triangles.

Monkey Wrench

Color	Shape	6"	9"	12"	15"
Black	A-1 square	2-1/2"	3-1/2"	4-1/2"	5-1/2"
	B-4 h/s triangles	2-7/8"	3-7/8"	4-7/8"	5-7/8"
	C-4 rectangles	1-1/2" x 2-1/2"	2" x 3-1/2"	2-1/2" x 4-1/2"	3" x 5-1/2"
Orange	B-4 h/s triangles	2-7/8"	3-7/8"	4-7/8"	5-7/8"
	C-4 rectangles	1-1/2" x 2-1/2"	2" x 3-1/2"	2-1/2" x 4-1/2"	3" x 5-1/2"

Mosaic Star

Color	Shape	6"	9"	12"	15"
Cream	A-4 h/s triangles	2-7/8"	3-7/8"	4-7/8"	5-7/8"
	B-8 q/s triangles	3-1/4"	4-1/4"	5-1/4"	6-1/4"
	D-1 square	2"	2-5/8"	3-3/8"	4"
Dk. Blue	A-4 h/s triangles	2-7/8"	3-7/8"	4-7/8"	5-7/8"
Purple	B-8 q/s triangles	3-1/4"	4-1/4"	5-1/4"	6-1/4"
Lt. Blue	C-4 h/s triangles	1-7/8"	2-3/8"	2-7/8"	3-3/8"

Mystery Garden

Color	Shape	6"	9"	12"	15"
Green	C-4 h/s triangles	2-7/8"	3-7/8"	4-7/8"	5-7/8"
Yellow	A-1 square	2-1/2"	3-1/2"	4-1/2"	5-1/2"
	B-8 q/s triangles	3-1/4"	4-1/4"	5-1/4"	6-1/4"
Orange	B-8 q/s triangles	3-1/4"	4-1/4"	5-1/4"	6-1/4"
Lt. Blue	B-4 q/s triangles	3-1/4"	4-1/4"	5-1/4"	6-1/4"
Dk. Blue	B-4 q/s triangles	3-1/4"	4-1/4"	5-1/4"	6-1/4"

Nine Patch

Color	Shape	3"	6"	9"	12"
Cream	A-4 squares	1-1/2"	2-1/2"	3-1/2"	4-1/2"
Red	A-5 squares	1-1/2"	2-1/2"	3-1/2"	4-1/2"

Ohio Star

Color	Shape	6"	9"	12"	15"
Cream	A-5 squares	2-1/2"	3-1/2"	4-1/2"	5-1/2"
	B-4 q/s triangles	3-1/4"	4-1/4"	5-1/4"	6-1/4"
Blue	B-8 q/s triangles	3-1/4"	4-1/4"	5-1/4"	6-1/4"
Red	B-4 q/s triangles	3-1/4"	4-1/4"	5-1/4"	6-1/4"

See page 132 for h/s and q/s cutting instructions

Sharing Blocks

Old Crow

Color	Shape	6"	9"	12"	15"
Cream	A-2 squares	2-1/2"	3-1/2"	4-1/2"	5-1/2"
	B-16 h/s triangles	1-7/8"	2-3/8"	2-7/8"	3-3/8"
	C-2 squares	1-1/2"	2"	2-1/2"	3"
Black	A-2 squares	2-1/2"	3-1/2"	4-1/2"	5-1/2"
	B-16 h/s triangles	1-7/8"	2-3/8"	2-7/8"	3-3/8"
	C-2 squares	1-1/2"	2"	2-1/2"	3"

Old Maid's Puzzle

Color	Shape	6"	9"	12"	15"
Green	A-3 squares	2-1/2"	3-1/2"	4-1/2"	5-1/2"
	B-6 h/s triangles	2-7/8"	3-7/8"	4-7/8"	5-7/8"
Gold	B-6 h/s triangles	2-7/8"	3-7/8"	4-7/8"	5-7/8"

Path Through The Woods

Color	Shape	6"	8"	10"	12"
Cream	A-1 h/s triangles	5-3/8"	6-7/8"	8-3/8"	9-7/8"
	B-7 h/s triangles	2-3/8"	2-7/8"	3-3/8"	3-7/8"
Brown	A-1 h/s triangles	5-3/8"	6-7/8"	8-3/8"	9-7/8"
	B-7 h/s triangles	2-3/8"	2-7/8"	3-3/8"	3-7/8"

See page 132 for h/s and q/s cutting instructions

Pinwheel

Color	Shape	4"	5"	6"	8"
Blue	A-4 h/s triangles	2-7/8"	3-3/8"	3-7/8"	4-7/8"
Gold	A-4 h/s triangles	2-7/8"	3-3/8"	3-7/8"	4-7/8"

Railroad Crossing

Color	Shape	4"	6"	8"	10"	12"
Cream	A-4 squares	1-1/2"	2"	2-1/2"	3"	3-1/2"
	B-2 h/s triangles	2-7/8"	3-7/8"	4-7/8"	5-7/8"	6-7/8"
Red	A-4 squares	1-1/2"	2"	2-1/2"	3"	3-1/2"
Black	B-2 h/s triangles	2-7/8"	3-7/8"	4-7/8"	5-7/8"	6-7/8"

Roman Square

Color	Shape	9"	18"
Cream	A-1 square	3-1/2"	6-1/2"
	B-8 rectangles	1-1/2 x 3-1/2"	2-1/2" x 6-1/2"
Brown	B-4 rectangles	1-1/2" x 3-1/2"	2-1/2" x 6-1/2"
Gold	B-4 rectangles	1-1/2" x 3-1/2"	2-1/2" x 6-1/2"
Black	B-4 rectangles	1-1/2" x 3-1/2"	2-1/2" x 6-1/2"
Rust	B-4 rectangles	1-1/2" x 3-1/2"	2-1/2" x 6-1/2"

See page 132 for h/s and q/s cutting instructions

Sharing Blocks

Sawtooth Star

Color	Shape	6"	8"	10"	12"
Tan	A-4 squares	2"	2-1/2"	3"	3-1/2"
	C-4 q/s triangles	4-1/4"	5-1/4"	6-1/4"	7-1/4"
Red	B-8 h/s triangles	2-3/8"	2-7/8"	3-3/8"	3-7/8"
Blue	D-1 square	3-1/2"	4-1/2"	5-1/2"	6-1/2"

Shoofly

Color	Shape	6"	9"	12"	15"
Blue	A-1 square	2-1/2"	3-1/2"	4-1/2"	5-1/2"
	B-4 h/s triangles	2-7/8"	3-7/8"	4-7/8"	5-7/8"
Green	A-4 squares	2-1/2"	3-1/2"	4-1/2"	5-1/2"
	B-4 h/s triangles	2-7/8"	3-7/8"	4-7/8"	5-7/8"

Sister's Choice

Color	Shape	5"	7-1/2"	10"	15"
Cream	A-8 squares	1-1/2"	2"	2-1/2"	3-1/2"
	B-8 h/s triangles	1-7/8"	2-3/8"	2-7/8"	3-7/8"
Pink	A-9 squares	1-1/2"	2"	2-1/2"	3-1/2"
	B-8 h/s triangles	1-7/8"	2-3/8"	2-7/8"	3-7/8"

See page 132 for h/s and q/s cutting instructions

Sharing Blocks

Spin City

Color	Shape	6"	8"	9"	10:	12"
Tan	A-4 h/s triangles	3-7/8"	4-7/8"	5-3/8"	5-7/8"	6-7/8"
Black	B-8 h/s triangles	2-3/8"	2-7/8"	3-1/8"	3-3/8"	3-7/8"
Orange	C-4 squares	2"	2-1/2"	2-3/4"	3"	3-1/2"

Star at Dawn

Color	Shape	6"	8"	10"	12"
Cream	A-6 squares	2"	2-1/2"	3"	3-1/2"
	B-10 h/s triangles	2-3/8"	2-7/8"	3-3/8"	3-7/8"
Purple	B-10 h/s triangles	2-3/8"	2-7/8"	3-3/8"	3-7/8"

Sugar Basket

Color	Shape	6"	8"	10"	12"
Cream	A-2 h/s triangles	3-7/8"	4-7/8"	5-7/8"	6-7/8"
	B-4 h/s triangles	2-3/8"	2-7/8"	3-3/8"	3-7/8"
	C-2 rectangles	2" x 3-1/2"	2-1/2" x 4-1/2"	3 x 5-1/2"	3-1/2" x 6-1/2"
Pink	B-4 h/s triangles	2-3/8"	2-7/8"	3-3/8"	3-7/8"
	D-1 square	2"	2-1/2"	3"	3-1/2"
Purple	A-1 h/s triangle	3-7/8"	4-7/8"	5-7/8"	6-7/8"
	B-2 h/s triangles	2-3/8"	2-7/8"	3-3/8"	3-7/8"

See page 132 for h/s and q/s cutting instructions

Sharing Blocks

Summer Winds

Color	Shape	6"	9"	12"	15"
Yellow	B-20 h/s triangles	1-7/8"	2-3/8"	2-7/8"	3-3/8"
	D-4 rectangles	1-1/2" x 2-1/2"	2" x 3-1/2"	2-1/2" x 4-1/2"	3" x 5-1/2"
Green	A-4 squares	1-1/2"	2"	2-1/2"	3-1/2"
	C-4 q/s triangles	3-1/4"	4-1/4"	5-1/4"	6-1/4"

This & That

Color	Shape	6"	8"	10"	12"
Cream	A-1 square	3-1/2"	4-1/2"	5-1/2"	6-1/2"
Lt. Blue	B-4 h/s triangles	3"	3-3/4"	4-1/2"	5-1/8"
Dk. Blue	C-4 h/s triangles	3-7/8"	4-7/8"	5-7/8"	6-7/8"

Cutting Instructions
Half-Sqaare (h/s) and Quarter-Square (q/s) Triangles

Half-Square Triangles
1. Cut a square the size indicated in the pattern.
2. Cut the square in half once diagonally for two half-square triangles.

Quarter-Square Triangles
1. Cut a square the size indicated in the pattern.
2. Cut the square into quarters diagonally for four quarter-square triangles.

General Instructions

For Every Project:

Here are some guidelines for gathering your materials for each of the projects in this book:

- For best results use good quality 100% cotton fabrics. These should measure between 42" and 44" wide.

- Scraps of fabric are intended to be those that you have on hand. If you should need to purchase these, 1/8 yard pieces or fat eighths will work, unless noted otherwise. See the size chart below for sizes of fabrics:

1/8 yard cut	4 1/2" x 44" rectangle
Fat Eighth	9" x 22" rectangle
1/4 yard cut	9" x 44" rectangle
Fat Quarter	18" x 22" rectangle

- If you prefer you may pre-wash fabrics for these projects, but it is not necessary. It is a good idea to test red and other colored fabrics for bleeding. Place a scrap of fabric in a glass or bowl of hot water. If you see a color change in the water, you may want to pre-wash that particular fabric. You should rinse until the water runs clear, then line or machine dry and press.

- Use a rotary cutter, rotary ruler and mat to cut fabric strips. Cut the fabric strips into squares, rectangles and triangles as directed in each pattern.

- All seam allowances are 1/4" unless noted otherwise.

- Press seams in one direction following arrows if indicated. If no arrows are indicated, press seam towards the darker fabric.

Hand Appliqué:

- Using template plastic or freezer paper, trace around each appliqué shape and cut out.

- Draw around template onto right side of desired fabric using pencil, chalk pencil or washable sewing marker.

- Cut out appliqué 1/4" beyond traced line.

- If layers of appliqué are needed, begin working at the background and work forward.

- Using the drawn line as your guide, slip stitch the appliqué into place. Use your needle to fold under the seam allowance. Take a 1/8" stitch down through the background fabric. Bring the needle up through the fold of the appliqué catching a few threads of the appliqué fabric. Insert the needle as close as possible to where it came up and continue for the entire appliqué shape.

Machine Appliqué:

- Using lightweight fusible web, follow the manufacturer's instructions for tracing and fusing:

- Trace the appliqué shape onto the paper side of the fusible web. Cut the fusible web about 1/8" from the outside traced line.

- Fuse the pattern to the wrong side of desired fabric. Cut out on the traced line. Transfer any dashed placement lines to the fabric.

- Peel off the paper backing. Position the appliqué on the background fabric, overlapping the pieces at the dashed lines. Fuse in place. Machine stitch using a zig-zag or buttonhole stitch.

Finishing the quilted projects:

Layering

- Cut the backing and batting 4" to 6" inches larger than the finished quilt top.

- Lay backing wrong side up on a smooth flat surface. Secure the edges with tape. Center the batting over the backing. Smooth the batting out. Layer the quilt top in the center of the batting. Smooth the quilt top out.

- Baste with large running stitches or small safety pins every 4". Begin in the middle and work out to the edges.

- Trim edges of the batting and backing even with the quilt top after the quilting has been completed.

Quilting By Hand

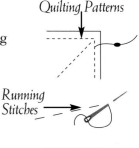

Quilting Patterns

Running Stitches

- Using hand quilting thread, thread a quilting needle with an 18" length of thread. Tie a small knot at the end. Insert the needle through the quilt top and into batting about 1" from where you want to begin quilting. Bring the needle up at the beginning of the quilting line. Give the thread a gentle tug to pull the knot through the quilt top and down into the batting.

- Take several small running stitches at a time, keeping stitches even and as close together as possible (1/8" to 1/4").

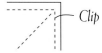

Clip

- To end a line of stitching, make a small knot close to the fabric. Insert the needle into the fabric and bring it out again about 1" from the end of the stitching. Pop the knot through the quilt top into the batting and clip the thread close to the quilt top.

Quilting By Machine

- Check your sewing machine manual for help with these tips:

- Use a walking foot for straight stitching of quilting lines. This will help to keep all layers of the quilt even. Pivot the fabric by keeping the needle in the down position when changing directions.

- Quilting stencils may be used for all types of designs. The embroidery or darning foot and lowering the feed dogs is helpful for this style of quilting.

Cross-Grain Binding

- Cut 2-1/2" x 44" strips of fabric. Cut enough strips to fit the outside edge of your finished quilt. Allow extra length to allow for diagonal piecing.

- Diagonally piece strips together.

- Fold Cross-Grain Binding in half lengthwise, wrong sides together and press.

Diagonally Stitch — *Trim to a 1/4" Seam Allowance* — *Press Seam Open*

- Unfold Cross-Grain Binding and fold down strip at 45° angle. Trim off even. Refold and press strip.

← Trim

- Align the raw edges of the Cross-Grain Binding on the top of the quilt at the trimmed edge. Pin if desired. Using a walking foot, stitch with a 3/8" seam allowance, starting 2" from the angled end.

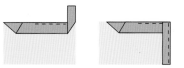

- To miter the Cross-Grain Binding at the corners, stop stitching 3/8" from the corner of the quilt top. Pivot and stitch off the edge of the quilt.

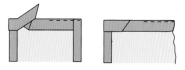

- Fold the Cross-Grain Binding up along the stitched line. Then fold the Cross-Grain Binding back down and even with the corner edge of the quilt. Begin stitching at the edge. Repeat to miter all corners of the quilt.

- Continue around the outside of the quilt working your way back to the beginning. Trim the end of the Cross-Grain Binding and tuck it into folded angled edge. Sew through all layers.

- Fold the Cross-Grain Binding around to the backside of the quilt and slip stitch into place, just covering the stitching line.

Fabric Swap Ladies

Courtesy of (L-R): Cindy Ohmart, Diane Crawford, Jill Reber